Job Descriptions

in Manufacturing

Industries

JOHN D. ULERY

Job Descriptions in Manufacturing Industries

A Division of American Management Associations

To my wife, Lorraine

Library of Congress Cataloging in Publication Data

Ulery, John D.
   Job descriptions in manufacturing industries.

   1. Job descriptions. 2. Job analysis. I. Title.
HF5549.5.J6U43   658.3'06   81-66223
ISBN 0-8144-5710-X   AACR2

First Printing

Preface

The Equal Employment Opportunity Commission is currently engaged in studies, through the National Academy of Sciences, to determine whether appropriate job measurement procedures exist or can be developed to assess the worth of jobs. Although the interim report only attempts to provide a descriptive review of the leading conventional approaches to job evaluation, it is quite conceivable the federal government will become actively involved in determining pay equity within any given organization.

In my opinion, any job evaluation plan must start with the job description. It is difficult, at best, to assign a wage or salary without a thorough understanding of an employee's expected duties and responsibilities. The National Research Council shares this opinion. In its *Job Evaluation: An Analytic Review*, the Council states, "the first step in the job evaluation process typically involves a careful description of each job within the unit being evaluated."

What the Council has failed to realize thus far, though, is that most organizations do not have job descriptions and that a lack of understanding on the part of those evaluating jobs and the employer's inability to explain grade and salary assignments rationally to employees have, in effect, led to Equal Employment Opportunity Commission involvement.

The purpose of this book is to assist employers to define the duties and responsibilities of their employees by way of job description examples, enabling them to be prepared for whatever form of job evaluation the federal government deems acceptable.

The job descriptions selected for this book are of typical benchmark jobs for any manufacturing organization.

Acknowledgments

I shall remain indebted to Bill Getch, Allied Chemical's Compensation Manager, for sharing his vast knowledge and wisdom with me in the field of compensation management. From conducting a manufacturing plant audit to developing an organization structure, he is one of the very best. Among many other things, Bill taught me the fundamentals of a properly written job description.

Bob Wilds, my last immediate supervisor at Allied Chemical, deserves special thanks for his patience with me in the formative years and his confidence in me in the later years.

John D. Ulery

Contents

PART ONE

Understanding
the Job Description

Use of the Job Description

With the Equal Employment Opportunity Commission's continuing involvement in job evaluation, it is only logical to assume that the importance of job descriptions will soon be discovered. No job evaluation committee or individual is capable of evaluating a job without a comprehensive knowledge of its duties and responsibilities. For this reason, job descriptions will be as important to companies in the 1980s as affirmative action plans were in the 1970s. Properly written descriptions have served and will continue to serve many useful purposes other than job evaluation. The following are just a few ways in which descriptions can be used.

Long-Range Planning. As an organization becomes larger, the mechanics of growth are more visible when job descriptions are written properly. An employer can determine where additional staffing is needed and which employees have the relevant education and experience to grow with the company.

Organization Structure. Properly written position descriptions can help an employer to identify duplication of efforts or determine if a function could be handled more efficiently and profitably elsewhere.

Communication. In the communication process between employer and employee, job descriptions can be an effective tool. The description gives the employee a reasonable understanding of what is expected. All too often, employees drift along doing what they deem proper, only to discover at salary review time that they have not been doing the job their supervisors expected. Managers, too, can benefit by seeing their responsibilities in writing. Outlining responsibilities for salary administration and/or

3

affirmative action in the job description will make Managers more sensitive to what senior management expects.

Employment. With a properly written description at the Recruiter's disposal, he or she is better equipped not only to prescreen applicants who do not have the proper education and/or previous work experience, but also to define intelligently what will be expected in the job to applicants who are interviewed.

Orientation. With descriptions, no one will start working without understanding what is expected in terms of relationships, duties, and responsibilities.

Performance Appraisal. With a properly written job description, it becomes much easier to evaluate an employee's performance. Comparing what an employee has accomplished to what was listed in the description is not nearly as subjective as trying to evaluate "attitude" or "appearance."

Training and Development. As an organization grows, job descriptions enable the employer to identify additional training and development needs for those employees designated as promotable.

Clarification of Relationships. With a properly written job description, employees will know exactly where they stand within the organization. They will not only know what others are responsible for and who is accountable to whom, but they will also have a much better understanding of how work is to be coordinated throughout the organization.

Compliance with Government Regulations. With properly written descriptions, an employer has a strong defense against potential discrimination charges or lawsuits against hiring practices if he or she has been consistent in the application of educational and experience requirements.

Establishment of Lines of Progression. The descriptions establish career ladders and lines of progression for employees, allowing them to set goals and objectives for themselves.

Termination. With each description in writing and properly communicated to the employee, an employer can easily establish evidence of inadequate work.

Preparation of Job Descriptions

For descriptions to be meaningful, they should be developed jointly by the Supervisor and the incumbent. The descriptions should also be updated at least annually or whenever the position has been changed significantly.

Perhaps the best mechanism for developing a description is a questionnaire filled out by the incumbent. Position analysis questionnaires can take many forms, but relevant sections should always include:

> *Basic Responsibility.* A brief statement defining the overall purpose and objectives of the job.
>
> *Primary Duties.* A basic outline of the kinds of duties performed to achieve the objectives.
>
> *Supervision Received.* A brief statement of the kind of supervision normally received by the incumbent.
>
> *Regular Contacts.* A brief statement describing internal and external contacts required in the job. Frequency, nature, and complexity of the contacts should be considered.
>
> *Supervision.* A brief statement describing type of supervision the incumbent is required to administer, and over what group of employees.
>
> *Requirements.* A brief statement describing minimum levels of education and work experience required to do the job.

Employees must be made to understand that the questionnaire is not a mechanism for determining "right or wrong" or intended to serve as a source of criticism. Its purpose is as a tool for both the employer and the incumbent to help determine a fair and equitable salary, and that purpose must be communicated to the employee.

After the incumbent has completed the questionnaire, the immediate supervisor should review it and make additions or deletions, discussing them with the employee. This version then becomes a mutual contract between the incumbent and the supervisor and is finalized by review and approval of the department head and/or the Personnel Department. Any significant

5

changes should be referred to the job evaluation committee or appropriate persons for possible upgrading or downgrading of the position salary grade.

The questionnaire will serve as a control mechanism over what employees are actually allowed to do in their jobs. Management may decide, for example, that it is not sound policy to have a secretary making employment decisions. The questionnaire will also help to determine whether the incumbent is exempt or nonexempt under the Fair Labor Standards Act.

Mutual understanding and agreement on duties and responsibilities are essential to the job evaluation and performance appraisal processes. All too often, an employee is hired to perform in one capacity and finds the position evolving into something much bigger because of that employee's capabilities. Without some form of control, preferably through the job description, employees can become quite disenchanted and seek other employment or even relief through the courts. Communication to the employee about his or her role in the organization is a must.

When the questionnaire has been completed, reviewed, and approved, we recommend that the rewrite or editing be completed by one person to achieve consistency and clarity. This person should normally be the Compensation Specialist, the Job Analyst, or someone specifically trained in job description writing.

Consistency in titles and job specifications is the prime consideration of the Job Analyst. A Foreman of Assembly in one plant, for example, should be called a Foreman of Assembly in another plant and have the same basic job duties and organizational relationships. Job specifications should also be identical for like jobs. The Foreman of Assembly in one plant should not be expected to have a Bachelor's Degree plus five years experience if the Foreman of Assembly in a comparable plant is expected to have a high school education and three years experience.

When the rewrite of the description has been completed, it should be distributed to all parties involved in the initial preparation for final signature. Incumbents should be encouraged to retain a copy and so should the supervisor, and both should be credited for their input. The final product will then be meaningful and one in which all involved can take pride.

Format of Job Descriptions

The actual format of the job description is strictly a matter of preference. One absolute necessity, however, is for the format to be consistent. Basic description format considerations should generally include:

1. *Identification Data*
    a. Division/department
    b. Location
    c. Name of incumbent
    d. Date
    e. Title of position
    f. Current salary grade
    g. Name of immediate supervisor
    h. Supervisor's title

2. *Basic Purpose*
    A few sentences that give a broad definition of the job and state its goals.

3. *Duties and Responsibilities*
    A listing of the duties and responsibilities of the job. This list should cover the major functional areas of responsibility and duties in order of relative importance. They should be listed in some detail in order to distinguish the job from others that may be closely related.

4. *Organizational Relationships*
    A description of all the relationships that help to locate the job's level in the organization. The superior and subordinate relationships are the key. Relationships to other jobs, individuals, or groups within or outside the organization are important.

5. *Functional Scope Data*
    A listing of the functional statistics commonly used in the industry and/or profession to indicate scope and size of responsibility. Examples are:

7

    a. Sales volume
    b. Total employment
    c. Operating budget
    d. Department payroll
    e. Total assets
    f. Number supervised, directly or indirectly
    g. Cost of rentals
    h. Purchasing volume
    i. Other

6. *Position Specifications*

The normal education or training required and the normal minimum experience required. All the foregoing should be regarded as being necessary for an average employee in order to attain a satisfactory level of proficiency in the job.

PART TWO

Examples of Exempt Job Descriptions

I

Administration

TITLE OF POSITION: **Vice-President, Personnel and Community Relations**

Basic Purpose

To direct and coordinate broad division activities having as their purpose the planning, development, and implementation of policies, programs, and practices in support of the employee relations, safety and loss prevention, community relations, pollution control, industrial hygiene, and medical affairs functions. To provide counsel and assistance to other division department heads and to other levels of management through specialized staff service departments.

Duties and Responsibilities

1. Assists the operating units with the selection, training, and development of executive, operation, and administrative personnel through staff departments.

2. Develops the basis for maintenance of the corporation's image in the view of employees, customers, shareholders, suppliers, and the general public.

3. Carries out to completion special projects and assignments in broad areas upon request of the President; meets regularly with the aforementioned to review progress and to reestablish priorities.

4. Manages and maintains a balanced organization possessing flexibility, maturity, and experience.

5. Develops and maintains an effective organization through selection, development, compensation, and motivation of managerial personnel; develops managerial and other talents necessary to achieve short- and long-range objectives by effective direc-

tion, counseling, and training according to an overall manpower plan.

6. Directs the development of and carrying out of approved affirmative action programs (AAPs) in the areas of Equal Employment Opportunity Commission (EEOC) compliance in accordance with the intent of Title VII of the Civil Rights Act of 1964.

7. Ensures administration, through subordinate managers, of programs for safety and loss prevention and environmental control consistent with the intent of the corporation's policy.

8. Selects, trains, develops, and organizes subordinate staff to use group and individual capabilities to maximum advantage.

9. Advises President of significant matters pertaining to labor difficulties, manpower shortages, and rate and benefit changes.

10. Supports the division Vice-President and Directors and other top-level executives in the achievement of their operational purposes by providing direct assistance or that of his or her staff functions or personnel.

11. Advises President of all facets of environmental control activities, including steps to be taken to reduce pollution at all operations, and interprets existing or proposed legislation and regulations. Reviews all capital projects to determine if environmental control considerations are adequate.

12. Represents the division before, and in its communication with, government air and water pollution control agencies.

13. Develops and directs a community relations program design to effect and improve understanding by employees and the public of the company's objectives and achievements.

14. Directs the preparation and release of publicity and maintains sound relations with the press, radio, television, and other media. Provides professional services to the executive staff of the division in speeches, letters, and articles that are to be made public. Coordinates activities with all appropriate corporate offices.

15. Directs the division's safety and loss prevention programs to assure conformity with corporate policy and federal, state, and local occupational safety and health negotiations. Assures that all federal and state reporting requirements are met on a timely basis.

16. Develops and maintains necessary medical departments

at various operating locations to assure sufficient first-aid treatment and appropriate medical evaluations for all employees. Makes certain that each location has adequate equipment and facilities to conduct the above functions.

17. Supervises appropriate personnel at operating locations to conduct periodic surveys of facilities to make certain that all plant and office conditions fall within acceptable industrial hygiene practices in accordance with federal, state, and division standards.

Organizational Relationships

This position reports directly to the President. Reporting to this position are the Director, Employee Relations; Manager, Safety and Loss Prevention; Manager, Environmental Services; Manager, Industrial Hygiene; Manager, Community Relations; and Director, Medical Affairs. Extensive contact with senior members of management of the division as well as corporate levels, including organization development, employee relations, and public relations.

Position Specifications

Bachelor's Degree in Business Administration or equivalent plus 12–15 years progressive experience in the employee relations discipline. Must possess extensive ability to communicate and display a high level of maturity and sound judgment.

TITLE OF POSITION: **Director, Industrial Relations**

Basic Purpose

To direct and coordinate broad division activities having as their purpose the planning, development, and implementation of policies, programs, and practices in support of the industrial relations, safety and loss prevention, security, and medical affairs functions. To provide counsel and assistance to other division department heads and to other levels of management.

13

Duties and Responsibilities

1. Assists the operating units with the selection, training, and development of executive, operation, and administrative personnel through staff departments.

2. Directs the development and carrying out of approved affirmative action plans in the areas of EEOC compliance in accordance with the intent of Title VII of the Civil Rights Act of 1964. Assures compliance on a divisionwide basis with state and federal mandates pertaining to EEO. Establishes realistic goals for affirmative action plans and provides support in achieving goals.

3. Ensures administration of programs for safety and loss prevention consistent with the intent of the corporation's policy. Assures that all federal, state, and local reporting requirements are met on a timely basis.

4. Selects, trains, develops, and organizes indirect staff to use group and individual capabilities to maximum advantage.

5. Advises Vice-President and General Manager of significant matters pertaining to labor difficulties; manpower shortages and future needs; wage, salary, and benefit changes; and similar problems.

6. Supports the division Vice-Presidents and Directors and other top-level executives in the achievement of their operational purposes by providing direct assistance.

7. Develops and maintains necessary medical departments at various operating locations to assure sufficient first-aid treatment and appropriate medical evaluations for all employees. Makes certain that each location has adequate equipment and facilities to conduct the above functions.

8. Provides counsel, guidance, and assistance and overall functional labor relations direction to all division locations in the administration, coordination, and interpretation of the corporation's and division's labor relations policies and objectives. Maintains an effective and appropriate union avoidance atmosphere at each facility.

9. Acts as company spokesman in the arbitration of disputes between employees and company at operating facilities.

10. Maintains liaison with corporate and local counsel in the disposition of labor charges and discrimination charges. Develops

company's position and formulates settlement terms where appropriate.

11. Directs various manpower programs, practices, and techniques, including recruitment and placement, organizational assessment and planning, employee performance appraisal, manpower inventories, and employee training and development to ensure adequate and qualified personnel at all levels.

12. Recommends changes in organization structure and manning requirements.

13. Participates in discussions and recommendations on divisional operating policies as a member of divisional general management, ensuring that sound industrial relations viewpoints are reflected.

14. Conducts periodic compensation studies and organizational analyses of division and plant locations to ensure proper and consistent grading of positions, titling of positions, and appropriate compensation for incumbents; ensures logical and meaningful lines of job progression for employees commensurate with sound compensation practices and company policies. Coordinates compensation studies with group industrial relations, submits to division management for approval, and oversees implementation when approved.

15. Counsels division and plant management on matters of organization and analyses as such activity relates to position evaluation and setting of salary grades, in order to maintain consistency and equity throughout the division.

16. Reviews proposed salary plans covering each division employee submitted annually by all locations; recommends to department heads the approval or disapproval of such forecasts, pointing out exceptions to salary administration guidelines and better salary administration practice; and recommends corrective action.

17. Directs the day-to-day implementation of the corporation's salary administration program within the division.

18. Directs the review of all salary administration control notices for completeness and timeliness, including verification of coding, salary grades, and titles; proper authorization and conformance to salary administration guidelines; and sound salary administration practices.

19. Makes certain that problems arising from unsatisfactory salary administration practices are resolved properly.

20. Manages and participates in the preparation of position descriptions, writing or rewriting as required; studies and analyzes position descriptions; evaluates positions to determine grades; audits position descriptions, evaluation of positions, and application of existing position classifications to individuals.

21. Directs the administration of all phases of hourly and salaried group life insurance, comprehensive medical insurance, stock purchase plan, educational assistance plan, sickness and accident insurance, long-term disability insurance, and accident insurance for active employees. Oversees the processing of necessary documents for implementation of these benefits. Resolves problem cases with individual employee or pensioner or insurance carriers.

22. Provides for orderly retirement of hourly and salaried employees, including counseling services to individual employees in advance of their retirement. Manages the review of hourly and salaried proposed retirements from plants and resolves nonconformance to policy with Personnel Managers or Plant Managers. Provides postretirement services and counseling to all retirees.

23. Ensures that all involuntary terminations throughout the division are consistent with sound industrial relations practices, serving as clearance point for all such actions.

24. Makes recommendations for improvements in wage and benefit programs consistent with the needs of the division.

25. Provides assistance to plant Personnel Managers in the conducting of wage and salary surveys and establishment of local area salary structures. Reviews local area surveys and recommends approval of resultant wage and salary structures.

26. Manages the maintenance of the census control program for the division and the issuance of monthly reports to division management.

27. Manages the preparation, maintenance, and timely distribution of organization charts for each location and division office.

28. Participates in activities of various professional organiza-

tions for purposes of exchanging industrial relations information and keeping up to date on the latest professional industrial relations developments.

29. Counsels and advises employees at all levels within the organization on personnel problems.

30. Coordinates the staffing activities of each location, including recruitment, layoff, recall, and termination of shop and salaried personnel, and personally engages in these activities when so required.

Organizational Relationships

This position reports to the Vice-President, Personnel and Community Relations. Reporting directly to this position are Managers of Labor Relations and EEO and Compensation and Benefits. Reporting functionally to this position are plant Personnel Managers. Extensive contact with senior levels of management.

Position Specifications

Bachelor's Degree, preferably in Business or Industrial Relations, plus 10–12 years of overall employee and labor relations experience, including managerial experience. Ability to maintain productive work relationships with various managerial levels— corporate, divisional, and plant.

TITLE OF POSITION: **Manager, Labor Relations and EEO**

Basic Purpose

To provide counsel, guidance, assistance, and overall functional labor relations direction to all division locations in the administration, coordination, and interpretation of the corporation's and division's labor relations policies and objectives. To maintain an effective and appropriate labor relations atmosphere at all organized operating facilities.

To ensure compliance on a divisionwide basis with state and

federal mandates pertaining to EEO; to establish realistic goals for EEO affirmative action plans and to provide support in achieving goals.

Duties and Responsibilities

1. Manages all division location activities in the planning and preparation for negotiations involving collective bargaining agreements, including all supplementary information and wage and fringe benefit surveys.

2. Participates in negotiations either as a spokesman at the bargaining table, as a backroom adviser, or in any other appropriate manner; keeps the Director and other interested levels of divisional and corporate management advised as to progress of negotiations.

3. Informs division plant locations of developments in labor legislation for compliance.

4. Develops and maintains contacts with international representatives.

5. Advises local representatives of interpretation of collective bargaining agreements and oversees proper administration of the provision of said agreements.

6. Manages activities of local representatives in matters pertaining to EEO, such as compliance reviews, affirmative action plans, charges of discrimination, and other related matters.

7. Develops positive plans to achieve company commitments. Advises local representatives of developments and current activities of the Commission and consequent impact on company plans and programs.

8. Acts as company spokesman in the arbitration of disputes between unions and company at operating facilities.

9. Maintains liaison with corporate and local counsel in the disposition of labor charges and discrimination charges. Develops company's position and formulates settlement terms, when appropriate.

10. Maintains liaison with corporate labor relations in all matters pertaining to collective bargaining and EEO to ensure that the division is in compliance with company objectives.

11. Ensures compliance with applicable laws and regula-

tions issued by OSHA, EPA, and other federal, state, and local regulatory agencies.

Organizational Relationships

Plant Personnel Managers report functionally in labor relations and EEO compliance matters. Meets and negotiates with international union representatives.

Position Specifications

Bachelor's Degree, preferably in Business Administration or Industrial Relations, plus 8–10 years of labor relations experience (negotiation, arbitration, contract administration).

TITLE OF POSITION: **Manager, Compensation and Benefits**

Basic Purpose

To plan, manage, coordinate, and interpret policies and procedures relative to the compensation function, including the processing of salary actions, absence with pay and terminal leave, and employee benefits and retirement, providing optimum service to all locations.

To coordinate division compensation and benefit activities with appropriate corporate offices.

Duties and Responsibilities

1. Conducts periodic compensation studies and organizational analyses of division and plant locations to ensure proper and consistent grading of positions, titling of positions, and appropriate compensation for incumbents; ensures logical and meaningful lines of job progression for employees within the unit commensurate with sound compensation practices and company policies.

2. Counsels division and plant management on matters of organization and analyses as such activity relates to position

evaluation and setting of salary grades, in order to maintain consistency and equity throughout the division.

3. Reviews proposed salary plans covering each division employee submitted annually by all locations; recommends to department heads the approval or disapproval of such forecasts, pointing out exceptions to the salary administration guidelines and better salary administration practice, and recommends corrective action.

4. Manages the day-to-day implementation of the corporation's salary administration program within the division.

5. Manages the review of all personnel change forms for completeness and timeliness, including verification of coding, salary grades and titles, proper authorization of and conformance to salary administration guidelines, and sound salary administration practices.

6. Ensures that problems arising from unsatisfactory salary administration practices are resolved properly.

7. Manages and participates in the preparation of position descriptions, writing or rewriting as required; studies and analyzes position descriptions; evaluates positions to determine grades; audits position descriptions, evaluation of positions, and application of existing position classifications to individuals. Reviews all changes of position title or salary grade.

8. Manages the administration of all phases of salaried group life insurance, comprehensive medical insurance, dental plan, stock purchase and savings plan, educational assistance plan, long-term disability insurance, and accident insurance for active employees. Supervises the processing of necessary documents for implementation of these benefits. Resolves problem cases with individual employee or pensioner, insurance department, and insurance carriers.

9. Provides for orderly retirement of salaried employees at other than plant locations and for counseling services to individual employees in advance of their retirement. Manages the review of hourly and salaried proposed retirements from plants and resolves nonconformance to policy with plant Personnel Managers or Plant Managers. Provides postretirement services and counseling to all retirees.

10. Ensures that all involuntary terminations throughout the

division are consistent with the policy of the company, serving as clearance point for all such actions.

11. Makes recommendations for improvements in benefit programs consistent with the needs of the division.

12. Provides proper compensation consultation, advice, interpretation, and services on compensation matters to all levels with the division.

13. Provides assistance to plant compensation representative in the conducting of salary surveys and establishment of local area salary structures. Reviews local area salary surveys and recommends approval of resultant salary structures to senior management.

14. Manages the maintenance of the census control program for the division and the issuance of monthly reports to division management and to the corporate office.

15. Provides for the preparation of professional statistical compensation and EEO reports and studies, as required.

16. Manages the preparation, maintenance, and timely distribution of organization charts for all departments. Sees that plant locations also submit charts, as required.

17. Provides guidance and direction in the preparation of organization charts on a divisionwide basis.

18. Participates in activities of various professional organizations for purposes of exchanging compensation information and keeping up to date on the latest professional compensation developments.

19. May counsel and advise employees and department heads to the levels of supervisory and managerial employees on personnel problems brought to his or her attention.

20. Coordinates, establishes, or recommends formal compensation and employee benefits programs for new plants or locations acquired during mergers.

21. Acts as division representative at interdivisional compensation, employee benefits, and retirement meetings.

Organizational Relationships

Position reports to Division Director, Employee Relations. Direct working relationships with top management levels of the division, as well as Plant Managers. Functional coordination of plant Personnel Managers in compensation and benefit matters.

Position Specifications

Bachelor's Degree in Business or Personnel Administration, or equivalent, plus 8–10 years of overall compensation and benefits-related experience, including supervisory experience.

TITLE OF POSITION: **Manager, Environmental Services**

Basic Purpose

To develop, monitor, and engage in environmental programs, including air, water, and solid waste control, to ensure that plant locations are in compliance with all regulatory requirements. To provide technical guidance to each plant location relative to energy conservation.

Duties and Responsibilities

1. Maintains liaison, for plant locations, with federal, state, regional, and local environmental regulatory agencies.

2. Negotiates permits with regulatory agencies at the state, local, and regional levels and participates in key federal permit negotiations.

3. Interprets environmental regulations as they affect plants and provides recommendations to Plant Managers on compliance programs; follows up to ensure implementation of compliance procedures.

4. Prepares or reviews technical reports for forwarding to the appropriate agencies on abatement programs and permits.

5. Reviews all capital projects for environmental compliance; provides advice and counsel to division and corporate engineering on the technical and regulatory aspects of all capital projects.

6. Conducts periodic pollution control audits.

7. Reviews all environmental-related correspondence and releases to appropriate regulatory agencies.

8. Investigates environmental complaints and regulatory orders and citations. Prepares responses to the agencies involved.

9. Provides technical guidance to plant locations in the development of conceptual waste treatment designs. Monitors waste control abatement programs and develops detailed project schedules. Arranges for special outside consulting and/or testing.

10. Reviews current literature on pollution waste control technology and regulatory activity to keep abreast of developments.

11. Prepares permit applications for construction and operation of planned facilities. Anticipates need for future pollution control equipment. Prepares annual environmental capital projections.

12. Prepares detailed technical comments on proposed regulatory actions and disseminates to all concerned personnel.

13. Manages the preparation and monitoring of milestone progress reports as required by agency orders and permits. Attends agency hearings on regulations, permits, and the like. Prepares and presents statements of such hearings on behalf of a plant, a division, or the corporation, as authorized.

14. May prepare and present statements relative to the environmental services function at public hearings.

15. Develops programs and provides guidance or participates with plant locations in implementing employee training programs related to environmental matters.

16. Inspects and determines competence and reliability of outside waste disposal contractors.

17. Directs the development and implementation of affirmative action programs that are in compliance with the intent of Title VII of the Civil Rights Act of 1964.

18. Ensures compliance with applicable laws and regulations and product quality standards issued by OSHA, EPA, and other federal, state, and local regulatory agencies.

Organizational Relationships

This position reports directly to the Vice-President, Personnel and Community Relations. Works closely and coordinates activities with corporate legal and environmental services departments. Also, works closely with outside agencies and associations to ensure compliance with environmental laws and regulations.

Position Specifications

Bachelor's Degree in Chemical Engineering, Chemistry, or Environmental Engineering or equivalent, plus 8–10 years related experience, including plant pollution control experience. Requires tact, diplomacy, and negotiating ability in dealing with various levels of management and regulatory agencies.

TITLE OF POSITION: **Personnel Manager, Plant**

Basic Purpose

To develop and maintain an employee relations climate that creates and permits a stable and productive workforce. To manage and coordinate all functions of employee relations, including employment, labor relations, compensation and benefit services, manpower planning, training and development, affirmative action, and security.

Duties and Responsibilities

1. Selects, trains, develops, and organizes a subordinate staff to perform and meet department responsibilities and objectives effectively.

2. Provides leadership in the establishment and maintenance of employee relations that will assist in attracting and retaining a desirable and productive labor force.

3. Manages the interpretation and application of established corporate and division personnel policies.

4. Directs the preparation and maintenance of reports necessary to carry out functions of the department. Prepares periodic reports for the Plant Manager; Director, Employee Relations; Manager, Labor Relations; and/or Manager, Compensation and Benefits, as necessary or requested.

5. Directs and maintains various activities designed to achieve and maintain a high level of employee morale.

6. Plans, implements, and maintains a program of orientation for new employees.

7. Provides and serves as the necessary liaison between the location employees and the location Plant Manager.

8. Supervises the labor relations staff in administration of the labor agreements and interpretation of contract language and ensures that the Supervisor, Labor Relations is well informed to administer the provisions effectively and in accordance with management's philosophy and objectives.

9. Strives to establish an effective working relationship with union representatives to resolve and minimize labor problems more satisfactorily and to avoid inefficient practices and work stoppages.

10. Determines, or in questionable cases recommends, whether grievance cases appealed to the arbitration stage should be settled by concessions or arbitrated. Prepares and presents such cases or supervises subordinates in same.

11. Manages and coordinates planning for plant labor contract negotiations; ensures that labor cost aspects are defined and that major position papers are prepared. Supervises the preparation and publication of contract language and documentation. Serves as chief spokesman or assists in negotiations at the operating unit level.

12. Establishes operative procedures for ensuring timely compliance with notice, reporting, and similar obligations under agreements with labor organizations.

13. Supervises the compensation and benefits staff in the administration and/or implementation and communication of current and new compensation and benefit programs, policies, and procedures.

14. Directs the development and implementation of approved location affirmative action plans to achieve and maintain compliance in accordance with the letter and intent of equal employment opportunity laws and executive orders.

15. Plans, implements, and maintains supervisory and management development activities.

16. Provides leadership in the establishment and maintenance of a plant security force.

17. Represents the company in the community and promotes the company's goodwill interests in community activities.

Organizational Relationships

This position reports directly to the Plant Manager and functionally to the Director, Employee Relations. Directly supervises Supervisor, Labor Relations; Supervisor, Employment; Supervisor, Compensation and Benefits; and Supervisor, Security; and indirectly supervises additional nonexempt employees. Interfaces daily with management and division employee relations.

Position Specifications

Bachelor's Degree, preferably in Personnel Management or equivalent plus 6–8 years related experience, including supervisory/managerial experience in a wide range of employee relations activities. Must possess an ability to understand human behavior and be able to lead and motivate people. Must have mature judgment and decision-making ability.

TITLE OF POSITION: **Supervisor, Labor Relations**

Basic Purpose

To establish, maintain, supervise, and coordinate an effective labor and employee relations program. To maintain fair and consistent administration and application of the labor agreements. To utilize programs and techniques to promote high morale, company loyalty, safety, and a stable and productive workforce.

Duties and Responsibilities

1. Supervises and coordinates labor relations activities. Provides leadership to develop, establish, and maintain a labor relations activity that assists in attracting and retaining a desirable and productive labor force.

26

2. Designs, implements, and maintains activities to establish, promote, and maintain a high level of employee morale.

3. Establishes and prepares operative procedures to ensure compliance with labor contract agreements.

4. Coordinates daily employee relations activities to minimize employee complaints and grievances and ensure prompt and fair settlement of employee complaints and grievances that do arise.

5. Interprets the labor agreements and advises management in application of labor agreements.

6. Selects, trains, develops, and organizes a staff to use group and individual capabilities to maximum advantage.

7. Develops, implements, and conducts supervisory training programs in labor relations subject matters.

8. Serves as liaison among hourly employees, union representatives, and location management and division employee relations.

9. Directs supervision in matters of hourly employee discipline, absentee control, grievances, and other similar problems. Prepares policies and procedures related thereto.

10. Serves as company spokesman at grievance meetings.

11. Recommends whether grievances appealed to arbitration should be settled or arbitrated. Prepares and presents arbitration cases.

12. Develops sound working relationships with union business agents, officers, and stewards.

13. Supervises the employee relations activities involving plant manpower levels, hourly employee benefits other than group insurance, leaves of absence, reference checks by other employers, unemployment compensation, hourly personnel record maintenance, and labor relations.

14. Assists with preparation for labor contract negotiations and serves on company negotiations committees. May act as spokesman.

15. Develops hourly training programs.

16. Oversees the tool and die make apprenticeship program, including ensurance of compliance with Title VII and other EEO requirements.

17. Ensures compliance with Title VII and other EEO legislation as applicable in labor relations activities and as applicable to the labor relations staff.

18. Reviews and analyzes labor law changes and new developments in the labor relations field as to effect upon location.

Organizational Relationships

Reports to plant Personnel Manager. Directly supervises two Specialists, Labor Relations; one Specialist, Manpower Planning; and four Clerks. Responsibilities frequently involve coordination of various labor and employee relations activities with the plant and department managers and/or their staffs.

Position Specifications

Bachelor's Degree in Personnel Management or a related field of study or equivalent and minimum of five years of varied practical experience in employee relations work, including minimum of three years in labor relations in a unionized plant. Good verbal and written communication skills needed. Must demonstrate sound judgment in the settlement of grievances.

TITLE OF POSITION: **Supervisor, Compensation and Benefits**

Basic Purpose

To coordinate and interpret policies and procedures relative to the salary compensation function, including the processing of salary actions, leaves of absence, severance agreements, terminations, employee benefits, and pension applications, and to supervise administrative activities related thereto.

Duties and Responsibilities

1. Coordinates various compensation studies with division compensation services; makes recommendations to plant management; oversees implementation when approved.

2. Reviews and assists in the preparation of annual proposed

salary plans by all departments; recommends to department heads and supervision the approval or disapproval of such forecasts. Advises on justification for exceptions to the salary administration guidelines and the most acceptable salary administration practices and recommends actions or initiates actions as appropriate to prevent or to correct salary administration problems and inequities.

3. Supervises the day-to-day implementation of corporate salary administration policies within the plant, including verification of coding, salary grades and titles, proper authorization of and conformance to salary administration guidelines, and sound salary administration practices.

4. Advises on appropriate salary offers to applicants based on qualifications, relative salaries in the plant, job market, and corporate salary guidelines and policies.

5. Supervises and participates in the preparation of position descriptions on proposed and revised positions.

6. Supervises the administration of all phases of salaried and hourly group life insurance, comprehensive medical insurance, dental plan, stock purchase and savings plan, educational assistance plan, long-term disability insurance, and weekly indemnity insurance. Oversees the processing of necessary documents for implementation of benefit changes and processing of benefit claims. Resolves problem cases with individual employee or pensioner and insurance carrier.

7. Reviews insurance claim experience to detect cases of questionable eligibility and failure to exercise coordination of benefits under hospital and medical plans, and instructs insurance carriers to investigate such suspected claims.

8. Prepares pension input data and calculations in accordance with corporate directives.

9. Provides for the orderly retirement of hourly and salaried employees and counseling services to individual employees in advance of their retirement. Provides postretirement service and counseling to all retirees.

10. Provides consultation, advice, and interpretation of policy and rules on discipline of salaried employees to all levels of supervision.

11. Supervises the maintenance of the census control program and the issuance of monthly reports to location and division management.

12. Ensures that personnel requisitions are properly completed within the scope of policy, that appropriate supporting documents are attached, and that they are forwarded for required approvals and recorded. Traces status when delays occur.

13. Manages the preparation, maintenance, and timely distribution of organization charts.

14. Participates in activities of various professional organizations for purposes of exchanging compensation information and keeping current on the latest professional compensation developments.

15. May counsel and advise salaried employees on personnel problems brought to his or her attention.

16. Coordinates the selection of personnel for attendance at corporate or in-house training as required.

Organizational Relationships

This position reports to the plant Personnel Manager. Maintains close working relationships with all levels of supervision and maintains open lines of communication with all salaried employees.

Position Specifications

Bachelor's Degree in Business Administration or equivalent, plus a minimum of four years experience in various phases of personnel functions, including at least two years experience in compensation and benefits. Communicates effectively both orally and in writing.

TITLE OF POSITION: **Supervisor, Security**

Basic Purpose

To provide basic plant security controls to protect employees, manufacturing plants, and company properly. Trains and supervises plant security guard force, conducts on-site investigations, and maintains liaison and good relations with local and state law enforcement agencies.

Duties and Responsibilities
1. Instructs and supervises the plant security forces.
2. Trains the plant security forces in job performance areas of access control, traffic control, physical security, fire surveillance, and emergency procedures.
3. Conducts physical security surveys of plant sites, submits written report(s) or surveys with recommendations to improve present or implement new measures at the locations. Prepares and implements internal and external security procedures (and measures) as directed.
4. Coordinates employee identification program to ensure that only authorized personnel enter plant. Also maintains visitor and vehicle logging procedure to ensure authorized entry only and to verify exit.
5. Investigates alleged in-house incidents of drug and narcotic abuse, alcohol use (intoxication), misappropriation and theft of company property, vending machine theft, theft of personal property, bomb threats, arson, and violations of security procedures, and submits written reports when appropriate or as directed by supervisor.
6. Maintains liaison with local and state law enforcement officials and agencies to achieve their cooperation and assistance as needed.

Organizational Relationships
Reports directly to plant Personnel Manager. Supervises security guards. Has a wide variety of contacts with both supervisory and nonsupervisory personnel for the coordination of activities and resolution of problems.

Position Specifications
Prefer an Associate Degree in Criminal Justice or equivalent. Requires minimum of four years of applicable experience in physical security and investigation. Must be capable of making mature and sound decisions under stress.

TITLE OF POSITION: **Supervisor, Environmental Control**

Basic Purpose

To plan and coordinate all plant activities related to the prevention or abatement of air and water pollution resulting from the operation of the facility.

Duties and Responsibilities

1. Obtains, analyzes, and evaluates a wide variety of data in order to assess potential air and water pollution sources accurately.

2. Recommends courses of action to remedy any noncompliance with environmental laws and regulations. Initiates corrective action upon approval.

3. Ensures a working knowledge of existing environmental control rules, policies, regulations, and laws and disseminates such information applicable to the plant in a clear and concise manner.

4. Communicates with local, state, and federal agencies to stay abreast of proposed and new regulations and to achieve an effective working relationship with such agencies.

5. Designs and/or reviews designs by others of a wide variety of environmental control systems, such as phosphate washers, air-purifying equipment, valve control equipment, chemical storage facilities, and related equipment. Inspects and/or supervises the installation of such equipment accordingly.

6. Evaluates all chemicals proposed for use at the facility to ensure their environmental safety, compatibility, and economic treatability before use.

7. Monitors facility discharges and emissions for compliance within required limits. Supervises plant effluent pretreatment operation to achieve the most effective and economical operation. Evaluates pretreatment equipment and operating procedures and adjusts accordingly.

8. Coordinates activities with production supervision to establish limits on the volume of wastes to the pretreatment operation to avoid conditions above the maximum allowable limits.

9. Develops, supervises, and maintains own department in order to accomplish the required objectives. Compensates, motivates, and disciplines subordinates in accordance with division policies and procedures. Conducts merit reviews on a timely basis.

Organizational Relationships

Reports directly to the Manager, Administrative Services. Interacts with all production departments and frequently consults and coordinates activities with division and corporate environmental services. Normally serves as company representative in business relationships with city, county, state, and federal environmental agencies.

Position Specifications

Bachelor's Degree in Engineering with environmental training or the equivalent plus 3–5 years related experience. Must have a working knowledge of chemistry, equipment specification and design, and construction practices.

TITLE OF POSITION: **Supervisor, Employee Relations**

Basic Purpose

To supervise assigned phases of the employee relations function, including administration of the labor agreement, policies and procedures concerning salaried and hourly benefit programs, and all phases of employment and manpower planning. To establish and maintain effective programs and controls in the areas of safety, environment, and workmen's compensation for compliance with federal and state regulations.

Duties and Responsibilities

1. Reviews and recommends disciplinary action concerning the hourly workforce.

2. Prepares documentation of grievances for employer/union meetings and arbitration.

3. Participates in grievance meetings and arbitration between the company and the union.

4. Cultivates information sources among employees to determine the pulse of the labor force.

5. Recruits and interviews salaried and hourly applicants to meet staffing requirements.

6. Recommends advertising when necessary in local and out-of-town newspapers and other publications as appropriate. Prepares advertisements.

7. Supervises the administration of all phases of salaried and hourly group life insurance, comprehensive medical insurance, weekly indemnity insurance, dental plan, long-term disability insurance, and educational assistance plan.

8. Resolves problem cases with individual employees and insurance carriers. Administers provisions of the labor agreement and maintain records as required.

9. Supervises the maintenance of hourly personnel records.

10. Approves personnel transactions on hourly employees.

11. Supervises the maintenance of an up-to-date seniority, layoff, and recall list; census report; and leave of absence.

12. Represents the company at all unemployment compensation claims hearings and appeals.

13. Participates in activites of various professional organizations for the purpose of exchanging information and keeping current on the latest professional developments relating to employee relations.

14. Provides assistance to plant Personnel Manager in conducting salaried and hourly surveys and establishing local area salary structures.

15. Provides assistance to plant Personnel Manager in the preparation of yearly affirmative action programs and investigates complaints concerning charges of discrimination.

16. Ensures that plant operates in compliance with federal and corporate safety and environmental policies.

17. Administers loss prevention programs to include proper equipment usage, fire prevention periodic audits, and follow-up investigations.

18. Maintains effective and professional first-aid station to

advise and assist employees with minor illnesses and injuries.

19. Administers workmen's compensation benefits.

Organizational Relationships

This position reports to the plant Personnel Manager. Reporting to this position is the Industrial Nurse; a Specialist, Safety; and a Senior Clerk, Employee Relations. Maintains close working relationship with all levels of supervision and maintains open lines of communication with all employees.

Position Specifications

Prefer Bachelor's Degree or equivalent plus 3–5 years personnel experience in an organized manufacturing environment.

TITLE OF POSITION: **Supervisor, Safety**

Basic Purpose

To plan, organize, and control the safety function of the plant to ensure that an effective accident prevention program is maintained and that appropriate measures are taken to comply with corporate, OSHA, and related safety policies and directives.

Duties and Responsibilities

1. Supervises periodic inspections of plant machinery, equipment, and working conditions to ensure conformance to appropriate safety and sanitary standards and regulations.

2. Examines plant equipment slated for purchase and proposed facility modifications and additions for safety requirements. Recommends modifications or adjustments to correct any deficiencies prior to purchase or use.

3. Determines appropriate safety equipment and safe work practices to be employed on specific jobs based on OSHA and corporate standards and implements accordingly through plant management.

4. Observes workers and work practices to ensure that protective devices and safe work procedures are used.

5. Coordinates activities with industrial hygiene personnel to maintain safe procedures involving toxic fumes, explosive air mixtures, and other hazardous circumstances that may be present and that cannot reasonably be eliminated.

6. Monitors, on a regular basis, the availability and condition of appropriate fire-fighting and safety equipment in the plant. Acts as liaison with companies servicing fire alarm system and fire extinguishers and with the local fire department.

7. Initiates and ensures investigations of accidents and unsafe working conditions, compiling statistical data and providing remedial actions to achieve effective accident prevention and avoidance of losses.

8. Chairs regular safety meetings and ensures that coordinated safety training and motivational campaigns are conducted in association with company policies.

9. Acts as liaison with government agencies and serves as plant management representative in case of inquiries and inspections to correct deficiencies and to minimize citations and fines for noncompliance.

10. Administers the worker's compensation insurance program through close coordination with the insurance carrier to minimize unnecessary lost work time by employees and unjust claims. Maintains close follow-up with employees or family members of those employees who may have been seriously injured while at work.

11. Acts as plant liaison with inspectors of insurance carriers. Determines management's position on inspectors' recommendations and prepares written response accordingly.

12. Keeps abreast of OSHA and corporate safety regulations and standards applicable to the plant. Communicates with and/or trains employees to the extent appropriate to achieve understanding and compliance of same. Develops and prepares plant safety procedures and rules, ensures their communication to those affected, and audits for compliance.

13. Provides assistance to supervisors regarding the evaluation of safety problems and of employee safety recommendations

and complaints. Determines acceptable corrective measures accordingly.

Organizational Relationships

Reports directly to the Manager, Administrative Services and has dotted-line responsibility to division and corporate Safety and Loss Managers. Provides safety expertise and direction to all levels of plant management. Has frequent contacts with representatives from OSHA and insurance carriers.

Position Specifications

Bachelor's Degree in Engineering with some emphasis in industrial safety programs or the equivalent, plus 5–7 years of related work experience. Must be capable of organizing effective accident prevention programs and conducting appropriate administration.

TITLE OF POSITION: **Specialist, Labor Relations**

Basic Purpose

To assist in coordinating and maintaining fair and consistent administration of collective bargaining agreements. To approve employee leave of absence requests and to administer disciplinary measures for violations of company rules and other acts of misconduct. To determine eligibility for holiday pay.

Duties and Responsibilities

1. Assists Supervisor, Labor Relations in coordinating labor and employee relations activities for the plant to minimize employee complaints and grievances and ensure prompt, fair settlement of complaints and grievances that arise.

2. Conducts disciplinary and other investigations. Administers discipline as necessary.

3. Attends grievance meetings and other company/union meetings as company representative.

4. Attends disciplinary and other investigative meetings as company representative.

5. Reviews holiday eligibility reports and determines employee eligibility for holiday pay.

6. Coordinates the service awards program for hourly employees.

7. Maintains and reviews employee leave of absence records, issuing letters of reprimand as necessary and taking more severe disciplinary action as individual situations warrant.

8. Reviews plant employees' attendance records to ensure that production departments are fairly and consistently enforcing the established guidelines.

9. Represents company at unemployment hearings.

10. Investigates grievances in preparation for advance steps of the grievance procedure, including arbitration.

11. Reviews matters of employee discipline, grievances, absentee control, and other employee relations matters with supervision.

12. Implements hourly employee training.

13. Assists with negotiation preparation; serves as member of negotiation committee.

14. Advises supervision on questions of company policy, rules and regulations, and contract compliance.

Organizational Relationships

Reports to Supervisor, Labor Relations. Coordinates various labor and employee relations functions with plant superintendents and other members of production supervision, quality control, engineering, safety, and payroll, and coordinates activities with other members of the personnel staff.

Position Specifications

Knowledge in the areas of human relations, labor relations, and employee discipline. Bachelor's Degree in Personnel Management or related field of study and two or more years practical experience in the employee relations discipline. Good verbal and written communication skills. Ability to work effectively with salaried and hourly employees. Mature; demonstrates sound and practical judgment.

TITLE OF POSITION: **Specialist, Manpower Planning**

Basic Purpose
　　To determine and coordinate employee reassignments, transfers, layoffs, and recalls and to achieve approved hourly workforce changes in accordance with the labor contracts. To verify vacation eligibility of hourly employees and process vacation requests.

Duties and Responsibilities
　　1. Fills hourly vacancies by transfer, job bid/award system, and/or recall of laid-off employees.
　　2. Curtails workforce by identifying employees to be reassigned, transferred, and laid off.
　　3. Posts job openings for bid, coordinates resulting transfers, and maintains job bid records.
　　4. Coordinates manpower changes with the plant production clerks and supervisory personnel.
　　5. Maintains up-to-date seniority roster of bargaining unit employees. Prepares and posts updated seniority listings at three-month intervals.
　　6. Maintains a layoff/recall index card file of bargaining unit employees.
　　7. Receives hourly employees' requests for vacation from all departments, verifying eligibility, and processes for preparation of vacation checks.
　　8. Assists Supervisor, Employment in interviewing and employment of hourly applicants as required.

Organizational Relationships
　　Communicates frequently with industrial engineering, plant superintendents, shift supervisors, and production clerks to coor-

dinate manpower changes. Reports directly to Supervisor, Labor Relations.

Position Specifications

High school diploma preferred or equivalent plus college or seminar courses in business administration or industrial relations helpful. One to two years experience in industrial relations with some understanding of seniority system. Ability to maintain orderly and accurate records. Mature judgment and tact needed in dealing with management and bargaining unit employees.

TITLE OF POSITION: **Specialist, Employment**

Basic Purpose

To recruit, interview, and select candidates for employment, ensuring timely replacement, effective orientation, and accomplishment of the plant's affirmative action goals.

Duties and Responsibilities

1. Recruits and interviews hourly and salaried (nonexempt) candidates. Selects all hourly candidates in unskilled and semi-skilled job categories; recommends candidates and schedules interviews with department supervisors for skilled and nonexempt salaried vacancies.

2. Plans hourly interview, preemployment physical, and orientation schedules to ensure that manpower needs can be met.

3. Develops effective recruitment sources to expedite filling employment vacancies and meeting AAP goals.

4. Conducts candidates' reference checks to include employment records, character, and safety habits.

5. Maintains hourly hire ledger, application log, and hourly employment application files.

6. Conducts orientation sessions with new hourly hires to familiarize them with working rules and benefits; also completes the necessary paperwork.

7. Prepares periodic reports on applicant flow; provides data

on hiring or rejection of minority, handicapped, and Vietnam-era veteran applicants.

Organizational Relationships

This position reports to the Supervisor, Employment and EEO. Frequent contact with various levels of management within the organization on employment and affirmative action matters.

Position Specifications

Bachelor's Degree in Business Administration or related field or equivalent plus minimum of one year experience in a comparable position. Must be able to communicate effectively, both orally and in writing.

TITLE OF POSITION: **Specialist, Safety**

Basic Purpose

To assist location safety manager in auditing and developing programs and to upgrade implemented accident prevention procedures and programs. To provide assistance in reviewing and maintaining records required by federal, state, and local laws, and by corporate directives and standards.

Duties and Responsibilities

1. Obtains and disseminates information regarding the safety program or individual procedures from resources of corporate, division, or other sources.

2. Observes and analyzes workforce performance with regard to safety and recommends specific measures, changes in procedures, or amendments to safety program.

3. Provides guidance to supervisors in the implementation of, adherence to, or stimulation of interest in the safety program.

4. Conducts monthly meetings of the plant safety committee and arranges agenda for the Plant Manager's supervisory safety meeting.

5. Organizes and coordinates training programs for all employees in first-aid and safety-related fields.

6. Makes regular plant safety and housekeeping inspections and issues reports to appropriate supervision.

7. Issues statistical data and reports covering accident performance.

8. Directs or participates in accident and near-miss incident investigations to determine causes so that recommendations for corrective action may be issued.

9. Indoctrinates new or transferred employees on safety policy and applicable safety rules.

10. Reviews and establishes safety glass program, stores safety equipment inventory and plant protective gear.

11. Serves as company representative on area industry emergency mutual-aid organization.

12. Assists in approving all engineering modifications or new construction for compliance with OSHA regulations.

13. Initiates requests for fire protection equipment.

14. Assists in training personnel in use of plant fire-fighting equipment and accessories.

Organizational Relationships

Reports to Manager, Plant Safety. Regularly assists line supervision with safety problems and training of employees. During absence of Manager, Safety, represents plant during inspections by representatives of government agencies, insurance carriers, and division and corporate offices.

Position Specifications

Degree in Industrial Safety or Hygiene, or high school graduate with minimum of two years experience in plant safety work. Must be capable of conducting safety meetings, detecting unsafe conditions and work practices, investigating accidents, and preparing reports.

TITLE OF POSITION: **Specialist, Industrial Hygiene**

Basic Purpose

To detect and monitor plant conditions that may adversely affect the health of employees and/or violate applicable laws, and to effect or recommend corrective measures.

Duties and Responsibilities

1. Identifies excessive noise exposures, potential or excessive air contaminant exposures, and hazardous chemical exposures based on appropriate tests and data. When excessive exposures are identified advises supervisor and initiates approved remedies.

2. Recommends securing assistance of division and corporate occupational health personnel and/or consultants when the necessary technical expertise is not available in the plant.

3. Helps evaluate feasibility and effectiveness of proposed measures to correct unacceptable health hazards and recommends final course of action. Effects and/or coordinates completion of approved corrective measures as assigned, and maintains records and documentation of remedial actions and results achieved that are related to health conditions in the plant.

4. Recommends or establishes, depending on the scope and effect, changes in work procedures, protective equipment requirements, and equipment standards (such as respirators, hearing protection, and protective clothing); drafts and recommends to supervisor written procedures and rules to protect the health of employees. Secures advice from division and corporate occupational health personnel as appropriate.

5. Advises Manager, Administrative Services of potential health hazards to employees and, as directed, conducts training for supervisors and employees on plant health matters such as protective equipment and chemical handling.

6. Supervises audiometric testing by technician of employees and new hires. Reviews and complies with recommendations of hearing conservation consultants or corporate specialists regarding retesting, work assignment restrictions, special hearing

protection, and so on. Coordinates as appropriate with employee relations and supervisors of employees.

7. Maintains file of current government occupational health laws and regulations and corporate directives; reviews and keeps current on requirements of those affecting this plant, including records and reporting requirements. Maintains required records, secures data for reports, and prepares required government and corporate reports for submission by department or plant manager.

8. Gathers data needed to evaluate merit of workmen's compensation claims related to occupational health areas, and assists in controlling and minimizing claims.

9. Reviews, as assigned, safety material data information on substances proposed for use in the plant and, on the basis of that information, recommends whether the substance can be present and used in the plant without endangering the health of the employees.

Organizational Relationships

This position reports to the Manager, Administrative Services. Maintains communications with plant Supervisor, Safety and plant supervisors and superintendents.

Position Specifications

Bachelor's Degree or equivalent training or experience in a science or engineering field. Minimum of one year experience or training related to industrial hygiene, safety, or chemistry required.

TITLE OF POSITION: **Industrial Nurse**

Basic Purpose

To administer immediate first-aid treatment to injured or sick employees and determine if they are physically able to work.

Duties and Responsibilities

1. Administers medication and treatment to sick and/or injured and reports and logs injuries and/or illnesses.

2. Maintains medical and workmen's compensation files that are up to date and accurate.

3. Issues safety equipment to employees and maintains files on payroll deductions concerning chargeable items.

4. Informs supervisor/foreman of employee's condition when sent to first aid (for example, sent home, sent to doctor, or sent to emergency room).

5. Takes call-ins for absences or tardies and informs immediate supervisor.

6. Documents first report of job-related injuries and illnesses.

7. Furnishes transportation for injured and/or sick to physician or hospital as needed.

8. Informs employees of medical leave of absence procedures and workmen's compensation procedures.

9. Provides follow-up care and advice to employees as appropriate.

10. Maintains log of occupational illnesses and injuries and prepares monthly OSHA report.

11. Reviews medical stock supplies periodically and ensures that adequate supply is on hand.

12. Types all correspondence as required.

13. Examines employees for employment purposes.

14. Refers employees to personal physician and/or social services if necessary.

Organizational Relationships

This position reports to the Supervisor, Safety.

Position Specifications

R.N. Degree. Prefer minimum of one year prior industrial experience.

Business Development

TITLE OF POSITION: **Vice-President, Business Development**

Basic Purpose

To develop and recommend division goals and criteria for the identification, evaluation, development, and marketing of new products and concepts to ensure the best utilization of the division's resources in accordance with its objectives for growth and profitability. To evalute, plan, implement, and assess the product market and to manage all aspects of product development through immediate subordinate directors to the point of actual manufacture. To recommend operational plans, spending levels, and staff requirements to achieve assigned responsibilities and to report achievements in relation to the plans.

Duties and Responsibilities

1. Seeks out, investigates, and assesses, in conjunction with appropriate corporate departments, business opportunities for the division developed internally or externally, including licenses, patents, joint ventures, acquisitions, and possible mergers.

2. Develops and administers a system for the review, approval, authorization, and control of proposed business ventures both internally and externally, including the technical, financial, and operational review of all programs and projects.

3. Evaluates the impact of new products on existing product lines and recommends actions to maximize profitability for the division.

4. Develops initial manufacturing plans, including expense budgeting and general administrative expense budgeting control programs for new business areas; prepares implementation procedures.

5. Assesses new product ideas from a marketing point of

47

view to determine feasibility, including analyzing market size and trends, gathering and appraising all available information on competitive products, preparing product description, getting data on price characteristics necessary to compete effectively in the market, getting estimates of sales and profit potential, assessing description of initial marketing plans and requirements, assessing manufacturing and technical feasibility and capital investment requirements, ensuring product performance from a consumer standpoint, and preparing a written summary report of new product ideas for review with the President.

6. Develops and recommends the marketing test programs for each new product in close cooperation with the Sales and Liaison Engineering Departments.

7. Prepares budgets and plans for preliminary test market.

8. Develops plans for measurement and projection of marketing tests to expanded distributions; completes the market test plans, including budgets, timing, location, and promotion schedule.

9. Recommends the final disposition of new and existing products in terms of abandonment, modification, further development, and/or testing of commercial marketing.

10. Manages the new product budget and periodically reports to the President on expenditures and operations versus plan.

11. Maintains an up-to-date knowledge of trends and developments in new products and processes in the industry, maintains liaison with research and product development groups, and participates in marketing and management seminars and associations.

12. Carries out special projects and assignments in broad areas upon request of the President; meets with the aforementioned to review and to reestablish priorities.

13. Manages and maintains a balanced organization possessing flexibility, maturity, and experience.

14. Develops and maintains an effective organization through selection, development, compensation, and motivation of assigned personnel; develops managerial and other talents necessary to achieve short- and long-range objectives by effective direction, counseling, and training according to an overall manpower plan.

15. Directs the development of and carrying out of approved AAPs in the areas of EEO compliance in accordance with the intent of Title VII of the Civil Rights Act of 1964.

Organizational Relationships

This position reports directly to the President. Extensive contact with senior members of management and corporate planning and business development, and regular contact with new and potential customers and vendors.

Position Specifications

Prefer Bachelor's Degree in Business Administration or Marketing plus 12–15 years related experience, including experience at a director or equivalent level. Requires maturity, tact, and diplomacy in dealing with various levels of management both within and outside the company. Requires excellent communicative ability (verbal and written).

TITLE OF POSITION: **General Manager, Business Development**

Basic Purpose

To develop plans and strategies for direction and administration of the division's new or proposed business activities. To formulate and recommend policies and programs for all assigned activities to ensure maximum sales volume at minimum cost and to maintain and improve the division's competitive position. To plan, direct, and coordinate all marketing and sales activities associated with the products.

Duties and Responsibilities

1. Directs the development of business plans and strategies consistent with short- and long-range objectives of the division and corporation.

2. Directs immediate subordinates in the management of their assigned areas to ensure that their responsibilities to attain objectives and satisfactory operation and performance are met in a

way that is consistent with established policies and programs.

3. Analyzes and appraises, regularly and systematically, the effectiveness of plant operations to ensure that established objectives will be met, that corporate and division policies are observed, and that prompt, corrective action is taken when necessary.

4. Develops and maintains an effective organization through selection, training, compensation, and motivation of all personnel.

5. Develops management talents necessary to obtain short- and long-range goals by effective direction, counseling, and training according to an overall manpower plan. Recommends approval of organization structure and manning requirements.

6. Reviews and evaluates contracts, appropriations, and expenditure requests submitted by immediate subordinates, approving those within authority and submitting those above authority to the Vice-President, Business Development with recommendations.

7. Determines and establishes, through joint consideration and planning, long- and short-term manufacturing objectives consistent with existing sales, projected sales forecasts, inventory requirements, and other factors involved.

8. Reviews reports on manufacturing activities, performance, and results and initiates action to correct deviations and variables as to schedules, excessive costs, material shortages, or other deterrent factors.

9. Recommends changes in existing policies necessary to the improved conduct of the business for the approval of the Vice-President or other higher levels of management.

10. Provides the preparation of accurate and reliable reports of current performance in the format and schedule agreed upon. Ensures that this information is communicated to the Vice-President and to those departments requiring it for division or corporate control, management reporting, or long-range planning.

11. Ensures that assigned departments meet objectives and conform to the policy guidelines of the division and corporation in areas other than return on investment and income growth. Objectives include maintaining satisfactory community and public relations, satisfactory employee relations, and safe operations of all facilities.

12. Coordinates work with division staff departments in the development of procedures, practices, and standards with which the new or proposed organization can function effectively, including sound accounting and financial administration; sound personnel practices and employee relations; sound practices for purchasing, distribution, and related services; and sound engineering, technical, and research programs for maximum utilization of division resources.

13. Directs the development of and carrying out of approved affirmative action programs in the areas of EEOC compliance in accordance with the intent of Title VII of the Civil Rights Act of 1964.

14. Assures compliance with applicable laws and regulations issued by OSHA, EPA, and other federal, state, and local regulatory agencies.

15. Develops and recommends pricing strategies based on evaluation of economic conditions, competition, and state and federal legislation that affect the marketability of the product. Participates in negotiations of product pricing agreements.

16. Maintains contact with operations and reviews procedures to appraise promptness of order processing and deliveries. Ensures quality of technical parts and services and other customer services.

17. Maintains favorable relations with all customers, including directing the administration of all promotional activities, and ensures that all customer entertainment is in line with corporate policy and procedures.

18. Seeks out, investigates, assesses, and recommends related new product applications.

19. Recommends the disposition of new and existing applications in terms of abandonment, modification, further development, and/or testing of commercial marketing.

20. Visits new and existing customers on a regular basis to maintain sound customer relations.

21. Carries out approved affirmative action plans for disabled veterans and veterans of the Vietnam era in accordance with the intent of the Vietnam Era Veteran's Readjustment Assistance Act of 1974.

Organizational Relationships

This position reports directly to the Vice-President, Business Development. Reporting to this position are the Plant Manager; Manager, Sales and Marketing; and one Product Engineer.

Position Specifications

Bachelor's Degree in Engineering or equivalent education/ work experience, including experience as a Plant Manager, plus 12–14 years broad engineering and manufacturing experience required. Must exercise sound judgment in all dealings and associations with customers.

TITLE OF POSITION: **Project Manager**

Basic Purpose

To conduct critical and advanced project research and development work on specific units and components of the product contributing to the total assignment or end product. To monitor the initial project and associated procedures required for the manufacture of new products.

Duties and Responsibilities

1. Evalutes the effectiveness of facilities for projected manufacturing schedules; ensures that dependable cost estimates are prepared to guide management in evaluating alternative proposals.

2. Participates with management in the development of short- and long-range plans for major layout changes; the preparation for increased production due to increased sales; and the incorporation of new processes, equipment, and other related matters. Expedites certain segments of projects to avoid costly delays, as authorized.

3. Directs the fabrication and refinement of working models prior to authorizing installation in production areas.

4. Provides systematic planning and coordination of services to achieve timely completion of major projects involving various

engineering changes, staffing, contractors, vendors, and other related services.

5. Participates with the Purchasing Department in the preparation of specifications and purchase orders that reflect acceptable quality, sufficient quantity, and delivery and service required to meet production schedules.

6. Ensures that materials, supplies, parts, and finished assemblies are transported and stored in an efficient and safe manner within the plant and that shipments are prepared in accordance with customer requirements.

7. Oversees feasibility studies for the fabrication of revised or new devices used in conjunction with the product.

8. Administers an ongoing safety control program and coordinates implementation requirements at new facilities.

9. Enters into technical discussions with customers, as requested.

10. Pursues projects aimed at substantial improvements in cost and quality of materials. Evaluates and investigates new equipment and processes on the market.

Organizational Relationships

This position reports to the General Manager, New Products.

Position Specifications

Bachelor's Degree in Mechanical or Electrical Engineering with 8–10 years experience in manufacturing, including experience in related plant design and maintenance activities.

TITLE OF POSITION: **Manager, Advanced Manufacturing Planning**

Basic Purpose

To organize, manage, and participate in the development of cost estimates for product, facilities, equipment, and staffing levels for a wide variety of new product systems. To interpret, explain, and justify cost estimates to top management personnel.

Duties and Responsibilities

1. Organizes and develops comprehensive cost estimates for new products. Evaluates and analyzes the design of each product to determine the most economical and functional systems, methods, and procedures for manufacture and appropriate tools, equipment, and facilities.

2. Determines and documents appropriate routing sheets, equipment lists, manning charts, skill level requirements, and plant layout for new product systems. Further evaluates and analyzes these products to determine facility costs and associated fixed and variable costs such as taxes, depreciation, and the like. Consults outside organizations and other sources to estimate and compile those costs.

3. Presents this comprehensive cost information to top management of division for evaluation. Interprets and justifies details of costs as required. Makes various adjustments to portions of cost estimate package in accordance with directions from management.

4. Prepares requisitions for equipment, tools, new facilities, refurbishment of existing facilities, utilities, and raw materials for new product systems.

5. Coordinates various adjustments such as engineering changes and related deviations with vendors as required.

6. Prepares comprehensive layout schedules and flow charts for new product systems, including such information as hiring schedules, delivery schedules, lead times, cash payment requirements, cost information, target production dates, start-up dates, and related information, and presents them to appropriate product manager. Attaches tooling lists, manning charts, summary of skill levels, and related schedules as required.

7. Provides technical assistance to New Product Manager by performing such functions as demonstrating new equipment to and instructing employees, documenting and setting up welding schedules, supervising all phases of plant layout, performing related applications, and other key start-up activities. Debugs new systems until they are totally operational.

8. Conceptualizes designs of test equipment and processes related to new products and provides these designs to tool and equipment design group for subsequent action.

9. Evaluates and analyzes costs and techniques of new concepts, disciplines, or applications for division products. Presents relevant data to senior management for further evaluation.

10. Develops, supervises, and maintains own department in order to attain the required objectives. Compensates, motivates, and disciplines subordinates in accordance with division policies and procedures. Conducts merit reviews on a timely basis.

11. Carries out approved affirmative action plans in the areas of Equal Employment Opportunity Commission compliance in accordance with the intent of Title VII of the Civil Rights Act of 1964.

Organizational Relationships

Reports directly to the Vice-President, Business Development. Continually interrelates with product engineering, quality assurance, and purchasing regarding the coordination of technical information. Interfaces with Controller's department for the interchange of information. Position has numerous outside contacts with engineering firms and a wide variety of vendors for the coordination of technical information. Position also has occasional contacts with corporate departments regarding environmental impact and equipment selection for chemical processing operations.

Position Specifications

Incumbent must have a Bachelor's Degree in Industrial Engineering or the equivalent plus 6–8 years related experience. Must have a comprehensive knowledge of equipment and tooling, metal cutting and finishing procedures, stamping, plating, heat treating, molding, and the characteristics of metal, plastics, textiles, and electronic components.

III

Controller's Group

TITLE OF POSITION: **Vice-President and Controller**

Basic Purpose

To plan, direct, and administer the division's financial affairs, including the treasury, Controller's, and planning and information systems functions to attain financial objectives based on division goals and policies. To formulate and recommend approval of policies and programs for the division's financial planning and analysis activities and coordinate the efforts of department personnel toward the reaching of goals.

Duties and Responsibilities

1. Develops and establishes objectives for the Controller's department consistent with division goals.

2. Develops, maintains, and directs an effective Controller's organization through selection, training, development, compensation, and motivation of all personnel. Approves or recommends approval of organization structures and manning requirements.

3. Directs the development and implementation of affirmative action programs that are in compliance with the intent of Title VII of the Civil Rights Act of 1964.

4. Formulates and recommends for approval proposals for policies on accounting, cost accounting, tax matters, the compilation of statistics and preparation of financial and cost reports, the control and protection of division inventories and other assets, the taking of physical inventories of properties and assets, and government reporting. Administers such policies when approved; establishes and administers procedures pertaining to above matters.

5. Advises and assists other members of management on mat-

57

ters pertaining to general accounting, cost accounting, and measurement of income and taxes.

6. Directs the activities of the Accounting Department in the preparation and maintenance of the division's accounting books and such other records as are necessary to the accomplishment of its functions.

7. Controls all the books of account of the division; keeps a true and accurate record of all property owned by it and of its debt, its revenue, and its expenses; keeps all accounting records of the division and renders to the division President, when required, an account of the financial condition of the division.

8. Directs the financial aspects of capital appropriation and expenditures in accordance with approved policies.

9. Formulates policies on credit matters and directs the credit and collection activities of the division's numerous facilities.

10. Formulates and recommends for approval proposals for policies on banking, borrowing, foreign currencies, receipt and disbursement of monies, and custodial and investment matters and on preparation and payment of payrolls; administers such policies when approved; and directs such activities for the division.

11. Conducts analysis of and recommends purchase or sale of securities and other investments.

12. Prepares such financial reports pertaining to treasury activities as are required or requested.

13. Negotiates and recommends execution of loans on behalf of the division.

14. Maintains advantageous relations with banks and other segments of the financial community.

15. Formulates and recommends for approval proposals for information systems and services policies and procedures for the division and for specific policies on development and operation of clerical and data processing systems within the division, including evaluation and recommendation for data processing and data communication equipment requirements, and administers such policies when approved. Directs such activities for the division.

16. Advises and assists other members of management on

matters pertaining to data processing, clerical systems, and management information.

17. Directs the activities of the Information Systems and Services Department in its development and review of systems, its data processing operations and research, its review of management information requirements, and its development and distribution of division policies and procedures.

18. Establishes and maintains a current plan of action, schedule of accomplishment, and assignment of resources relative to systemization objectives and progress toward implemention.

19. Exercises overall direction over the preparation and coordination of the division's strategic plan, capital plan, and profit and operational plan.

20. Develops and maintains procedures for strategic profit and capital planning and an effective system of budgetary control. Conducts the preparation of the plans in a manner designed to meet the requirements of management; conducts financial analyses as may be directed; assists in planning and decision making throughout the division through advice and consultation.

Organizational Relationships

Participates in discussions and recommendations of division policy operations as a member of the division's general management; ensures that sound financial viewpoints are reflected. Coordinates department's activities and maintains close liaison with corporate Controller's department, accounting, and cost accounting, which includes financial statements, measurement of income, taxes, internal and external audits, profit plans, and appropriations; Treasurer's department, which includes banking, investments, credit, borrowing, and other financial matters; Information Systems and Services Department on matters relating to the operation of these functions, including the development of overall management information systems; and the Corporate Planning and Business Development Departments, which includes the strategic, profit, operational, and capital plans.

Position Specifications

Bachelor's Degree, preferably in Accounting, Finance, or Business Administration, plus 12–14 years of diversified overall

59

financial experience, including related Assistant Controller's experience, needed. Should possess characteristics that show sound judgment in fulfilling position duties and responsibilities as well as in handling relationships with senior members of division management.

TITLE OF POSITION: **Assistant Controller**

Basic Purpose

To manage the development, interpretation, and reporting of financial information to support the attainment of division objectives. To establish accounting practices and procedures consistent with sound, generally accepted accounting principles, and in accordance with division and corporate policy.

Duties and Responsibilities

1. Manages the activities of the Accounting Department in the maintenance of the division's accounting books and such other records as are necessary to the accomplishment of its function. Monitors all books of account of the division's subsidiary companies by thorough examination of their financial statements.

2. Ensures adherence to sound, generally accepted accounting principles, such as the accurate matching of revenues and cost, sensible capital versus revenue decisions, conservative valuation of inventories and other assets, and consistency in the application of these and other principles.

3. Applies sound consolidation techniques in combining the financial statements of all the division's legal entities into single consolidated financial statements that reflect the earnings and financial condition of the entire division accurately. Analyzes and reports financial results to corporate and division management on a timely basis, providing data critical to the management decision-making process.

4. Manages the division's cost accounting activities, including establishing standards for all direct, variable manufacturing costs contained in the inventory, making accurate comparisons of

actual manufacturing costs with standard costs, and reporting resulting variances to management on a timely basis. Monitors the cost accounting activities in the division's European manufacturing locations to ensure adherence to sound accounting principles.

5. Oversees and assists in all accounting functions performed at the North American plant locations in accordance with division policies and procedures.

6. Formulates or recommends for approval proposals for policies on accounting, cost accounting, tax matters, the compilation of statistics and preparation of financial reports, control protection of division inventories and other assets, the taking of physical inventories of properties and assets, and government reporting. Formulates procedures to implement such policies when approved.

7. Administers certain areas of the treasury function; specifically, preparation of financial reports as required.

8. Acts as functional contact with the company's independent auditors on accounting matters.

9. Develops and maintains an effective organization through selection, development, compensation, and motivation of assigned personnel.

10. Manages the development of, and carrying out of, approved AAPs in the areas of EEOC compliance in accordance with the intent of Title VII of the Civil Rights Acts of 1964.

Organizational Relationships

This position reports to the Vice-President and Controller. Reporting to this position are the Supervisors of Financial Reporting, General Accounting, and Systems and Procedures. Provides functional direction to the plant Controllers. Maintains liaison with corporate Controller's department regarding accounting, cost accounting, financial statements, and measurement of income, taxes, and auditing.

Position Specifications

Bachelor's Degree in Accounting plus 8–10 years of experience in general accounting and cost accounting, including managerial experience, needed. Must have leadership and communicative skills and show sound judgment in performing duties and responsibilities.

TITLE OF POSITION: **Manager, Financial Planning and Analysis**

Basic Purpose

To plan, direct, and administer activities of the planning and financial analysis group including developing planning systems and procedures, analyzing and coordinating consolidation of financial estimates, and reviewing appropriation requests and other special business and economic studies.

Duties and Responsibilities

1. Develops and implements plans and systems to meet division and corporate requirements in the estimating of net income.

2. Develops short- and long-range business strategies and alternatives in conjunction with division management, including profit plans and ten-year strategic plans.

3. Works with division management in formulating business objectives and analyzing key actions and strategies to meet objectives set for each business area.

4. Manages and coordinates the preparation of written and oral presentation material of estimates and plans within the division.

5. Formulates, in conjunction with operating personnel, financial analyses of special projects, including analysis and preparation of major appropriation requests. Manages the activities of subordinates in the review, analysis, and control of routine appropriation requests.

6. Carries out special projects and assignments in broad financial and planning areas upon request of the Vice-President and Controller. Meets regularly with the aforementioned to review progress and to reestablish priorities.

7. Manages and maintains a balanced organization possessing flexibility, maturity, and experience through selection, development, compensation, and motivation.

8. Manages the development of and carrying out of approved AAPs in the areas of EEOC compliance with the intent of Title VII ot the Civil Rights Act of 1964.

Organizational Relationships

This position reports directly to the Vice-President and Controller. Reporting to this position are two Financial Analysts and one Clerk-Typist. Extensive contacts with Corporate Office Appropriations Department and Planning Department. Occasional contact with International Finance, Tax, Law, and Purchasing Departments. Coordinates work with operational personnel at several levels within the division in formulating plans and in obtaining estimates.

Position Specifications

Bachelor's Degree in Business Administration, Finance, or Accounting, or equivalent, plus 6–8 years related experience in financial planning and analysis, as well as supervisory experience, required.

TITLE OF POSITION: **Controller, Plant**

Basic Purpose

To plan, coordinate, and administer the plant accounting function, including cost accounting, general accounting, inventory accounting (production auditing and perpetual records on raw materials), payroll accounting, accounts payable, plant Information Systems and Services (IS&S), profit planning, earnings estimates, and other forecasts, taxes, special analyses, economic evaluations, and capital expenditure planning. To plan and oversee directly the taking of physical inventories, including the reconciliation and evaluation thereof.

Duties and Responsibilities

1. Maintains an effective plant accounting function in line with the Vice-President and Controller's approved organization.

2. Monitors the department procedures and controls in effect for consistency with division and corporate policies, procedures, and guidelines.

3. Provides direction and assistance in the preparation of annual profit and operational plans at the plant level.

4. Develops, implements, and monitors a system of statistical and cost reporting in line with division objectives.

5. Formulates and institutes procedures for plant physical inventories; oversees each actual inventory, verifies the count and evaluation, and records the results.

6. Performs special cost studies and/or analyses for location and division management. Reviews and advises Plant Manager of profitability of current product lines. Prepares manufacturing performance reports and provides for complete analysis of interpretation to location managers. Consolidates other accounting data and the preparation of statements utilized for management information.

7. Assists the Vice-President and Controller in the analysis of the financial status of the plant and in the preparation of recommendations with respect to future financial plans, forecasts, and policies.

8. Interprets, verifies, and delegates legal regulations, requirements, procedures, policies, and related concepts.

9. Provides assistance to the Vice-President and Controller on the research, analysis, and evaluation of matters and expedites such matters to conclusion when so directed.

10. Maintains, either directly or indirectly through subordinate supervisors, satisfaction of department staffing requirements, training, communicating, and conforming with such other requirements as are essential to the operation of the accounting function.

11. Assists Plant Manager and other plant management personnel on salaried manpower requirements, capital expenditures, major expense outlays, and other programs as they relate to plant operation.

12. Serves and participates on a wide variety of committees, including the energy committee, safety committee, and profit improvement committee.

13. Directs plant management in preparing earnings estimates and other forecasts relating to plant operation.

14. Conducts, and advises plant management with, daily, weekly, or monthly meetings on manufacturing cost variances.

15. Advises and counsels various managers of other departments on financial and nonfinancial matters as they relate to plant and division operation.

16. Maintains production auditing staff to ensure correct production and scrap reporting.

17. Develops, supervises, and maintains Accounting Department in order to reach the required objectives. Compensates, motivates, and disciplines subordinates in accordance with division policies and procedures. Conducts merit reviews on a timely basis.

18. Maintains perpetual records on certain raw materials to enable calculation of material usage.

19. Maintains material on consignment records to ensure proper usage at vendor's facilities.

20. Carries out approved affirmative action plans in the areas of EEOC compliance in accordance with the intent of the Civil Rights Act of 1964.

21. Confers with and assists staff personnel on day-to-day problems and procedures.

22. Keeps well informed and abreast of new developments in accounting and other financial areas through contact with educational institutions and professional societies and perusal of texts, technical papers, and periodicals.

Organizational Relationships

This position reports directly to the Plant Manager. Functional reporting relationship to the Vice-President and Controller. Reporting to this position are the Supervisors of Cost Accounting, Payroll Accounting, Vendor Accounting, Customer Accounting, and plant IS&S, and a Secretary.

Position Specifications

Bachelor's Degree in Economics or Business Administration, with a major in accounting or equivalent. Advanced courses in financial management, investments, business law, and electronic data processing beneficial. Eight to ten years of experience preferred to include preparatory accounting and supervisory positions to acquire sufficient background to assume responsibilities of the position.

TITLE OF POSITION: **Accountant, Plant**

Basic Purpose

To plan, coordinate, administer, and manage the plant's accounting functions in accordance with division and corporate policies and procedures, while utilizing generally accepted accounting practices. To formulate and direct the preparation of adequate cost reports for management. To coordinate the taking of physical inventories and the reconciliation and valuation thereof.

Duties and Responsibilities

1. Maintains an effective plant accounting organization, including the selection and training of accounting personnel who show a high degree of maturity, promise, creativity, and professionalism.

2. Establishes and maintains procedures and controls at the plant in order to develop accounting data consistent with division and corporate policies and guidelines, as well as adherence to sound, generally accepted accounting principles.

3. Develops and maintains cost and general accounting procedures and guidelines in accordance with division and corporate policies.

4. Formulates and institutes procedures for the direction and control of physical inventories, the adequacy of the physical count, and the valuation and recording of the results.

5. Maintains a system of production reporting to monitor inventory transactions.

6. Coordinates and controls manufacturing cost changes to ensure proper data input.

7. Ascertains that accounting policies and procedures are complied with by location personnel.

8. Maintains a system of scrap surveillance and reporting.

9. Supervises the preparation of the plant's profit and operating plan; monitors performance against the approved plan.

10. Supervises the preparation of the capital expenditures strategy plan and monitors performance against the approved plan.

11. Provides recurring estimates of revenue and expense for division and location management.

12. Represents plant in financial and tax matters with local institutions as required.

13. Adheres to and assists in maintaining spirit of corporation's EEO philosophy.

Organizational Relationships

This position reports to the Plant Manager. Reporting to this position are one exempt and three nonexempt employees. Reports functionally to the division Controller. Frequent contact with plant and division department heads.

Position Specifications

Bachelor's Degree in Accounting or equivalent education/ work experience, plus 5–7 years work experience in professional accounting positions required. Effective communication and supervisory skills essential. Maturity, initiative, and creativity in carrying out position's duties and responsibilities are essential.

TITLE OF POSITION: **Supervisor, Systems and Procedures**

Basic Purpose

To maintain and improve the division's financial systems by providing ongoing, independent review, appraisal, evaluation, and verification of accounting and financial and other operating controls and procedures established to safeguard the division's assets.

Duties and Responsibilities

1. Develops uniformity in operational reporting throughout the division and reviews such reports to ascertain their continued necessity; integrates various operating reports with other functional reports to determine consistency in reporting and to eliminate duplicate efforts.

2. Interfaces with division information systems and services to automate repetitive-type reports and to establish meaningful, comparative financial presentations for management. Oversees financial reporting and ensures proper development to that end.

3. Verifies that operating units of the division comply with accounting, financial, and other operating controls and procedures prescribed by the corporation; checks the reliability of the accounting and reporting system of the division through effective auditing of the aforementioned units.

4. Recommends establishing new or making improvements on existing financial, accounting, and other operating policies and procedures as disclosed through auditing activities and reports to the Assistant Divisional Controller the corrective action, or lack of corrective action, taken on the recommendations.

5. Reviews, edits, approves, and issues reports of audit findings and makes appropriate recommendations in such a manner that management may evaluate the matters covered in the report and take appropriate corrective action.

6. Reviews existing procedures to ascertain that the division's assets are safeguarded and that proper accountability and responsibility are clearly defined and maintained. Develops and publishes procedures to protect the division's assets where those procedures do not presently exist.

7. Formulates or recommends for approval proposals for policies on general accounting, cost accounting, the compilation of statistics, the review of financial reports, and the control and protection of division inventories.

8. Manages the development of, and carrying out of, ap-

proved AAPs in the area of EEOC compliance in accordance with the intent of Title VII of the Civil Rights Act of 1964.

Organizational Relationships
This position reports to the Assistant Divisional Controller. The incumbent is responsible for establishing and maintaining a cooperative relationship with both corporate and division management. This position contributes to the overall profitability of the division by providing a service to the company at an optimal cost and by making such cost improvement recommendations as are appropriate as disclosed by auditing activities.

Position Specifications
Bachelor's Degree in Accounting plus 3–5 years progressive experience in auditing, including supervisory experience. Must have leadership and communicative skills and demonstrate sound judgment in performing duties and meeting responsibilities.

TITLE OF POSITION: **Supervisor, Financial Reporting**

Basic Purpose
To supervise the preparation of consolidated financial statements and the preparation and distribution of all financial reports, including historical data, to division and corporate management.

Duties and Responsibilities
1. Supervises and assists in the preparation of the monthly consolidation of financial statements of the division's entities, applying sound, consistent accounting practices and ensuring timely and accurate reporting.
2. Supervises and assists in the preparation and analysis of financial results by business area. Coordinates the reporting activities of the various division entities, ensuring timely reporting to division and corporate personnel.
3. Coordinates and assists in the preparation and analysis of

financial variances and coordinates the timely reporting of operating variances by plant personnel.

4. Provides other financial and statistical information reports, such as tax, insurance, asset, and others required by corporate and division personnel.

5. Supervises and assists in the analysis and interpretation of the statements of the division's foreign subsidiaries for reasonableness and in certain cases directs the attention of management to areas requiring attention.

6. Reviews the activities of the domestic plant General Accounting departments to determine efficiency of operation and adherence to division and corporate policy.

7. Reviews and assists in the development of division general accounting policy and participates in the development and statement of sound procedures.

8. Completes special studies and other assignments as directed by the Assistant Controller.

9. Supervises the analysis of the U.S. dollar financial statements of the division's foreign subsidiary companies for reasonableness and conformity with generally accepted U.S. accounting principles.

10. Supervises the monthly consolidation of the financial statements of the division's legal entities, applying sound, consistent consolidation techniques, thus ensuring timely measurement of the division's earnings and an accurate statement of its financial position.

11. Supervises the preparation and analysis of financial results by business area, leading to the reporting of such data to division and corporate management in a clear, concise manner, with business explanations for variances obtained from operating personnel.

12. Maintains a high degree of professionalism and reliability within his or her area of responsibility by providing strong leadership, direction, motivation, and training.

13. Ensures compliance with the corporation's policies in the areas of affirmative action and equal employment opportunity in his or her area of responsibility by closely monitoring all personnel actions.

14. Develops, supervises, and maintains own department in

order to reach the required objectives. Compensates, motivates, and disciplines subordinates in accordance with division policies and procedures. Conducts merit reviews on a timely basis.

Organizational Relationships

Reports to the Assistant Controller. Direct supervision of three exempt employees. Has frequent contacts with personnel from the various plant Controller's departments, Accounting Supervisors, and corporate Controller's, Treasurer's, tax, and insurance personnel for the interchange of information.

Position Specifications

Bachelor's Degree with a major in Accounting or equivalent work experience. Four to six years experience in the industrial general accounting area or equivalent public accounting training. Must possess effective managerial and communication skills.

TITLE OF POSITION: **Supervisor, General Accounting**

Basic Purpose

To coordinate, plan, and supervise the general accounting services and functions for the division office in accordance with generally accepted accounting principles as well as corporate and division policy. To maintain a system of accounting and internal controls for the U.S. locations in the areas of tooling, fixed assets, engineering, and intercompany pricing.

Duties and Responsibilities

1. Supervises, coordinates, and assists in the performance of accounting services for the division office, including accounts payable and payment drafts, miscellaneous billing, travel advance and expense accounting, intercompany transfer pricing for products, tooling and services, engineering project accounting, and all other areas of expense necessary for the recording and reporting of expenses related to the division's activities.

2. Serves as a liaison among plants and division and corpo-

rate offices in the transfer of charges between locations, and directs and assists in the reconciliation of interlocation accounts.

3. Develops and implements procedures within the assigned area of responsibility.

4. Monitors the accounting for the North American tooling revenues, expenditures, and amortization. Analyzes and evaluates tooling projects and prepares a monthly tooling status report for the division management decision-making process.

5. Administers and controls retroactive selling price adjustment accounting, ensuring that adequate documentation for all accounting accruals is maintained.

6. Monitors and administers the engineering project accounting for the North American locations.

7. Performs special projects as assigned by the Assistant Controller, such as evaluating the costs of financial tooling and analyzing liability variations from previous month's balances.

8. Develops, supervises, and maintains own section in order to reach the required objectives. Motivates and disciplines subordinates in accordance with division policies and procedures. Conducts merit reviews on a timely basis. Ensures compliance with the corporation's policies on affirmative action and equal opportunity in his or her area of responsibility.

Organizational Relationships

This position reports to the Assistant Controller. Has frequent contact with personnel from the various plant Controller's and Accounting Departments and with corporate Payable, Receivable, Payroll, Controller's, and Tax Departments for the interchange of information.

Position Specifications

Bachelor's Degree in Accounting or equivalent plus 4–6 years of combined industrial and general accounting experience. The ability to communicate effectively with all levels of management and employees is important. Candidate should possess characteristics of sound judgment, initiative, and creativity in carrying out position responsibilities.

TITLE OF POSITION: **Cost Analyst**

Basic Purpose

To coordinate the valuation of the manufacturing routing file and assist division purchasing in the development of material standard costs for that file. To review, analyze, and prepare reports of sales/product cost and contribution for division and corporate management. To initiate improvements in the data discipline over the routing system and sales accounting system in keeping with division management objectives.

Duties and Responsibilities

1. Develops standard costs for material and parts based on historical and future purchasing practices for valuation of inventory and measurement of income.

2. Prepares IS&S input documents representing standard direct cost elements (material, labor, variable burden) developed by division and plant Controller's personnel to establish cost tables for the valuation of the manufacturing routing file.

3. Coordinates with the manufacturing administration group the updating and corrections required to the manufacturing routing file prior to the periodic recosting of the file.

4. Performs regular reviews and audits of the manufacturing routing file and coordinates with the plant Controller's and manufacturing group in the timely correction of errors and omissions (obsolete and incorrect routings) between the periodic recosting periods.

5. Reviews and audits the monthly sales/cost of sales detail prepared by plant accounting personnel and prepares the necessary journal entries and support for general ledger input.

6. Analyzes and prepares reports from the monthly sales/cost of sales detail showing the sales, product cost, and contribution by product line, including comparison with profit plan and prior year. Reports are prepared monthly and quarterly for division and corporate management.

7. Reviews and analyzes the periodic physical inventories of plants for possible obsolete and slow-moving material and pre-

pares reports directed to the plant Controllers for investigation.

8. Calculates the standard cost of routing additions and changes manually between the periodic recosting periods and prepares the IS&S input documents necessary to update the costed manufacturing routing file.

9. Directs the maintenance of the historical records of purchases of material and parts and the related files of purchase orders and price changes by the Senior Accounting Clerk.

10. Completes special projects as required in the area of cost accounting, such as the analysis of contribution differences on similar product lines and the analysis of cost differences on similar manufactured and purchased parts.

Organizational Relationships

Reports directly to Supervisor, Cost Accounting. Communicates with senior division Controller's department personnel. Interfaces with Supervisory Controller's department personnel on general accounting, planning, and IS&S matters. Advises plant cost accounting personnel. Consults with division and plant purchasing and industrial engineering personnel.

Position Specifications

Bachelor's Degree in Accounting or the equivalent plus 4–6 years of industrial accounting experience in standard direct cost systems with some background in general accounting. Ability to communicate with all levels of management. Some initiative and creativity in carrying out duties is important. Should demonstrate the potential to advance to a more responsible position.

TITLE OF POSITION: **General Accountant I**

Basic Purpose

To prepare and compile a variety of division accounting data, including construction-in-progress information, bank reconciliations, and related information. To issue monthly reports on this information accordingly.

Duties and Responsibilities

1. Codes all general orders of the U.S. division locations per established procedures and generally accepted accounting principles.

2. Compiles and issues monthly report, including each project number, amount spent to date, and the general order allotment. Indicates which projects are closed to fixed assets.

3. Contacts various plant location accounting personnel to ensure that all expenditures in general orders have been made. Transfers closed general orders to fixed capital.

4. Compiles data from ledgers and statements for management control reports, including such information as administrative and selling expenses, engineering costs, and fixed manufacturing costs.

5. Prepares bank reconciliations for the hourly payroll bank accounts.

6. Prepares schedules for fixed capital and depreciation charges and otherwise assists higher classified personnel in month-end accounting closing.

Organizational Relationships

Reports directly to the Supervisor, General Accounting. Has frequent contacts with accounting personnel from various plant locations regarding the interchange of information.

Position Specifications

Incumbent must have a Bachelor's Degree in Accounting or the equivalent.

TITLE OF POSITION: **General Accountant II**

Basic Purpose

To prepare consolidated financial statements. To participate in the maintenance of books of account, ensuring that all financial data are recorded in accordance with generally accepted accounting principles consistent with division and corporate policies.

Duties and Responsibilities

1. Produces monthly consolidated financial statements, financial results by legal entity, and various supporting schedules for corporate and division management, ensuring timely preparation and overall reasonableness. Participates in the maintenance of the division's accounting records and maintains adequate supporting documentation for all journal entries. Monitors and coordinates activity for the expense distribution of the salaried payroll by department.

2. Provides detailed financial reports as required by corporate bulletins or special corporate or division management requests. Coordinates and directs subsidiary company efforts relating to such reports.

3. Reviews and analyzes general ledger account balances for such items as accrued payroll accounts, accrued liabilities, accrued receivables, and income statement accounts. Isolates problem areas and recommends necessary corrections.

4. Organizes, directs, and controls the retention of historical accounting and legal records, ensuring that all information is safely stored and available on short notice.

5. Compiles data for the management control report, such as statements of source and disposition of funds and schedules supporting European indebtedness and various income statement items.

6. Prepares monthly reconciliations of the general ledger balance to the bank balance for hourly payroll bank accounts.

7. Prepares monthly consolidated reports in relation to the corporate standard reporting project. Analyzes and reviews corporate definitions and recommends account classification to the Supervisor, General Accounting.

8. Consults with accounting personnel to provide regular monthly reconciliation of intracompany accounts receivable and payable.

9. Provides assistance and financial information to internal and independent auditors.

10. Prepares other financial and statistical information requested by the Supervisor, General Accounting, such as trend analyses of sales and net income and accounts receivable trial balance detail.

Organizational Relationships

Reports directly to the Supervisor, General Accounting. Communicates regularly with other Controller's department personnel at the plant, division, and corporate levels. Interfaces occasionally with division management personnel.

Position Specifications

Bachelor's Degree in Accounting or equivalent plus 2–4 years experience in general accounting. Should possess the ability to communicate with all levels of management. Initiative and creativity in fulfilling duties are important. Should demonstrate the potential for advancement to a more responsible position.

TITLE OF POSITION: **Cost Accountant**

Basic Purpose

To perform routine and special cost analyses to support the plant manufacturing effort according to corporate, division, and local policies and procedures. To prepare various routine and special reports and analyses as requested to provide adequate and accurate manufacturing cost information. To prepare journal entries affecting manufacturing cost and inventory values.

Duties and Responsibilities

1. Prepares journal entries to record manufacturing cost and inventory valuation.

2. Prepares and analyzes various reports, as required or directed, relating to the financial performance of the manufacturing effort.

3. Analyzes and reports cost effects or manufacturing changes.

4. Performs special cost analyses as requested by superior to support local and division personnel.

5. Participates and assists in preparing recurring estimates of revenue and expense.

6. Participates and assists in taking and reconciling physical inventories.

7. Recommends and develops modifications and improved cost accounting techniques and methods.

8. Costs routing changes and prepares cost file changes.

9. Participates and assists in preparation and analysis of monthly financial statements.

10. Participates in the preparation of profit and operating plans, budgets, and supplementary supporting schedules.

11. Develops definitions and criteria regarding cost and budget philosophy for the proper definition and accurate tracking of manufacturing costs.

Organizational Relationships

Reports directly to Plant Controller. Has no direct subordinates. Has frequent contact with Plant Manager and other Managers in a data-gathering and consultative role. Regular day-to-day contact with other accounting functions, mechanical engineering, and division accounting is required in performing job functions.

Position Specifications

Bachelor's Degree in Accounting or Business Administration or equivalent education/work experience, with 3–5 years cost accountant experience in a manufacturing firm. Knowledge of budgeting, standard cost, and inventory valuation helpful. Substantial exposure to mechanical data systems and understanding of interrelationships of accounting, payables, payroll, and data processing necessary.

TITLE OF POSITION: **Financial Analyst**

Basic Purpose

To develop planning systems and procedures and perform independent analysis, interpretation, and consolidation of financial estimates. To prepare and review appropriation requests, conduct special business and economic studies, and compose necessary commentary on each, all to serve both division and corporate management requirements.

Duties and Responsibilities

1. Reviews and assesses validity of financial estimates from responsible sources, consolidates this information, and prepares detailed business commentary on projections of net income, capital expenditures, balance sheets, and cash flow for total division and each business activity on a periodic basis.

2. Prepares detailed requests for inputs; establishes time schedule; coordinates interface among marketing, manufacturing, and IS&S personnel with appropriate review of inputs; and consolidates wide range of operating and financial projection in the development of both short- and long-range business plans, including three-year profit plans and ten-year strategic plans.

3. Prepares necessary presentations, including comparisons with prior performance and projections for presentation to division and corporate management.

4. Prepares and issues appropriate schedules of the approved annual budget by month to responsible division management.

5. Outlines requirements and prepares associated request to responsible personnel, analyzes and reviews the results, and prepares appropriate written presentation for division management review on special projects, including appropriation requests, price strategy, and competitor strategy.

6. Designs and maintains necessary reporting system for division control of fixed capital appropriations and expenditures.

7. Issues request to responsible division personnel for data to respond to special and routine needs of the division in the corporation. Reviews and assembles the information in format suitable for division management review.

8. Monitors actual financial and operational data and their reporting in order to be consistent in presentation and commentary.

Organizational Relationships

This position reports directly to the Manager, Planning and Financial Analysis. Extensive contacts with division operating and staff personnel at all levels in fulfilling normal duties and responsibilities. Occasional contact with corporate office, primarily Controller's and Planning Departments.

Position Specifications

Bachelor's Degree in Business Administration, Finance, Accounting, a technical field, or the equivalent, plus 2–4 years direct experience in financial or operational analysis. Ability to communicate both in writing and orally with all levels of management. Some initiative and creativity in fulfilling duties is important. Should demonstrate the potential to advance to a more responsible position.

IV

Electronic Data Processing

TITLE OF POSITION: **Manager, Information Systems and Services**

Basic Purpose

To plan, organize, and manage the division's information systems and data processing activities to attain management systems objectives based on division goals and policies. To formulate, and recommend approval of, procedures and computer applications to solve business systems problems.

Duties and Responsiblities

1. Plans, coordinates, controls, and supervises the overall information systems and services of the division to fulfill the division's manpower and equipment requirements for efficient business systems.

2. Provides the IS&S resources necessary to support the on-going needs of division functions for the design, implementation, and processing of diverse business, engineering, and scientific systems.

3. Utilizes manpower and equipment resources through the application of motivating techniques and the delegation of responsibility and appropriate authority to subordinate Supervisors and project leader.

4. Plans, coordinates, and manages the activities involved in the study of business problems; the development and analysis of alternative solutions; and the programming, testing, implementation, computer processing, procedures, and forms design of the selected solution.

5. Participates on various steering committees and such other task forces as may be established by division management to plan, organize, and install major systems projects.

6. Reviews, in concert with user management, alternative

solutions and recommendations prepared by subordinate Supervisors and/or project leaders, to determine if proposed solutions are adequate to meet short- and long-term requirements, are compatible with equipment capacities, and are in accordance with acceptable techniques, workload, schedules, and operational costs.

7. Confers with user representatives when necessary to assist in resolving procedural difficulties, clarifying their responsibility and objectives, and establishing problem definitions.

8. Formulates and supervises department procedures and controls and ensures that division and corporate standards are maintained to provide control over project planning and the development of computer applications.

9. Ensures that current techniques of computer technology are considered in the development of problem solutions, but that the methods selected are the ones that provide the most efficient cost/performance ratio.

10. Administers all work rules, disciplinary actions, and employment practices, including those related to equal employment opportunities, personnel and management development, employee performance appraisals, and salary administration.

11. Manages and coordinates the preparation and distribution of the IS&S procedures manual.

12. Formulates, and recommends approval of, proposed operating expense and capital budgets, with appropriate documentation for the division Information Systems and Services Department, and analyzes and assists in the preparation of same for all plant information systems and services functions.

13. Manages the preparation of, and reviews, periodic reports required by division and corporate management with regard to computer operations, equipment, and manpower utilization and costs.

14. Coordinates the installation of packaged computer software products with vendor representatives and consultants. Ensures continuity of technical systems support following completion of vendor participation.

15. Provides assistance in the training of user personnel in understanding and fulfilling their individual responsibilities in the implementation and operation of new or revised systems.

16. Ensures that both division and plant information systems and services staff are provided with adequate technical training to enable them to fulfill their responsibilities.

17. Provides resources for the conduct of postinstallation systems audits and systems performance evaluations as measured against goals and objectives.

18. Monitors the data processing and data communications activities of the division's European and North American plant locations to ensure compatibility and adherence to division and corporate standards.

19. Provides adequate precautions in the design and processing of systems and the operation of division and plant data processing facilities to ensure the security of information, equipment, and access to data files.

Organizational Relationships

Reports to the Vice-President and Controller. Maintains close liaison with corporate Information Systems and Services Department on matters relating to the information systems design, programming and documentation, data processing operations, and data communications.

Position Specifications

Prefer Bachelor's Degree in Business Administration or Computer Science or equivalent education/work experience, plus 8–10 years progressive experience in data processing, systems design, and programming in a manufacturing environment. Must be capable of managing and motivating professional employees and possess leadership, communicative skills, and sound judgment.

TITLE OF POSITION: **Project Leader, Systems**

Basic Purpose

To plan, guide, design, and implement various computerized systems to meet user requirements in the areas of production and inventory control, payroll applications, general ledger systems, sales accounting or analysis, and the like.

Duties and Responsibilities

1. Reviews requests submitted by users to determine feasibility of computerizing a solution to particular user problems; investigates and gathers detailed information and recommends alternative solutions to the problems.

2. Develops logic flow charts of present systems to understand the interactions better in preparing design criteria of new systems.

3. Designs a system to satisfy the needs of the user, presents the system for approval, and develops detailed specifications for programming and job flow.

4. Estimates time requirements for programming and job flow development and distributes to appropriate systems development personnel for implementation.

5. Monitors the progress of systems development personnel in meeting target dates; determines reasons for not meeting target dates; and provides additional support or modifies completion date when user requirements have changed.

6. Conducts postaudits to ensure that original benefits of the system are still being reaped and recommends corrective action as necessary.

7. Advises Manager, Operations of any special or additional hardware/software required by the systems design.

8. Develops a user manual or set of user instructions alone or in conjunction with user originating request.

9. Provides for the ongoing development and supervision of subordinate programmers and/or programmer analysts through training and performance evaluation.

10. Coordinates the testing and schedules production of the various systems with the Manager, Operations.

11. May provide liaison between division IS&S group and computer manufacturers, software vendors, and the corporate IS&S group.

12. Prepares and submits management reports to the Manager, IS&S as required.

Organizational Relationships

This position reports to the Manager, Information Systems and Services. Reporting to this position are two Programmers and/or Programmer-Analysts. Coordinates day-to-day activities with the Manager, Computer Operations and the Manager, Systems Planning and Engineering. Frequently has contact with management throughout operations. May have occasional contact with corporate departments.

Position Specifications

Bachelor's Degree or equivalent required plus 4–6 years experience in systems design. Prefer prior supervisory experience. Must have a working knowledge of business administration, state-of-the-art computer hardware, data management techniques, and general business and/or manufacturing systems. Must keep abreast of latest developments in data processing field.

TITLE OF POSITION: **Supervisor, Computer Operations**

Basic Purpose

To supervise and be accountable for the efficient operation of computers and off-line units, including data entry, quality control, scheduling, production, and distribution.

Duties and Responsibilities

1. Reviews schedules and program instructions and assigns and instructs computer and equipment operators, using personnel skills and experience to obtain best operating efficiency, equipment utilization, and accuracy of results on standardized programs.

2. Interprets instructions, directs and assists operators in preparing computer and off-line units, and assists in the testing of new and revised programs.

3. Assists Systems Analysts in determining cause and/or rectifying computational and procedural errors in computer or other unit malfunctions.

4. Coordinates activities with various sections within the department on matters pertinent to the operation of the computer.

5. Participates in the planning and scheduling of the department's schedules and operations.

6. Maintains operating records and reference files and prepares reports as to operating time, equipment repair, service, and so on.

7. Maintains satisfaction of the section's requirements in the area of staffing and training of personnel.

8. Administers work rules and disciplinary action when warranted.

9. Appraises employee performance and recommends changes in status and wage adjustments.

10. Controls the security of the data processing and telex facilities and ensures that protective measures are provided for data and back-up processing.

11. Provides for the control of magnetic tapes and disk files and their retention.

12. Maintains control of the inventory of data processing operating supplies and controls operating expenses.

13. Ensures that all new and modified systems are supported with operating procedures in accordance with division standards.

14. Monitors the performance of individual applications within the data center and requests modifications to improve productivity and/or reliability.

15. Monitors performance of equipment and vendor's response to problems and recommends actions to improve productivity and reliability.

Organizational Relationships

This position reports to the Manager, Information Systems and Services. Supervises five to eight nonexempt personnel and is responsible for second-shift operations. Interacts with user management and plant IS&S functions throughout all locations. Has outside contact with vendors and technical representatives.

Position Specifications

High school graduate or equivalent with courses in business education and mathematics preferred. Post–high school courses

and training equivalent to two years of college on pertinent subjects, to include the operation of computers and associated off-line
equipment, are desirable. Three to five years experience required
to learn duties and nature of the work being processed, and to
become familiar with the system's logic and supervisory responsibilities.

TITLE OF POSITION: **Senior Programmer Analyst**

Basic Purpose

To define system, program, and job flow specifications developed by systems analysts and to produce meaningful and efficient logic programs and operating techniques to satisfy user requests. To supervise the technical performance of programmer
personnel.

Duties and Responsibilities

1. Designs, estimates time requirements, programs, and implements major changes to systems, programs, or job flow as requested by users.

2. Reviews specifications and time estimates to determine if
further clarification is required to produce results requested by
user.

3. Creates computer program logic to process data to achieve
meaningful output that will satisfy user request.

4. Prepares job control language (JCL) records to produce a
logically sound job stream that could comprise one or more activities.

5. Develops data record layouts, input forms and record formats, proposed report formats, testing schemes, and test data.

6. Makes use of software programs or routines provided by
computer manufacturer in areas of sort, utility, and bulk media
conversion, and other related areas.

7. Writes computer programs from logic flow charts, record
layouts, and input and report formats.

8. Desk checks program for obvious errors and has it

keypunched and compiled; creates JCL to test program, reviews output for correctness, and, if necessary, modifies program.

9. Assists computer operations personnel in implementing the productive running of jobs.

10. Formulates documentation for projects, operations, and program in accordance with corporate IS&S and division standards.

11. Creates permanent files as required on disk storage device.

Organizational Relationships

Reports directly to the Project Leader, Manufacturing Systems. Has occasional contacts with managers or supervisors from the various local departments to satisfy systems, program, or job flow requests. Has numerous contacts with computer operations and data conversion personnel to clarify data and procedures. Has limited travel. Supervises the activities of two Programmers/Programmer Analysts.

Position Specifications

Bachelor's Degree or equivalent plus 4–6 years experience in COBOL programming, with some systems design. Working knowledge of accounting or manufacturing systems and highly proficient in data management techniques, data communication concepts, and job control language. Must keep abreast of the latest techniques in the data processing industry, particularly when it affects programming and systems design.

TITLE OF POSITION: **Programmer Analyst**

Basic Purpose

To interpret systems, program, and job flow specifications developed by more highly classified personnel and to produce meaningful and efficient logic programs and operating techniques that will satisfy user requests. To design, program, and implement minor systems or modifications to systems, programs, or job flow to satisfy user requests.

Duties and Responsibilities

1. Designs, estimates time requirements, programs, and implements minor changes to systems, programs, or job flow as requested by users.

2. Reviews specifications and time estimates to determine if further clarification is required to produce results requested by user.

3. Creates computer program logic to process data to achieve meaningful output that will satisfy user request.

4. Prepares job control language (JCL) records to produce a logically sound job stream that could comprise one or more activities.

5. Develops data record layouts, input forms and record formats, proposed report formats, testing schemes, and test data.

6. Makes use of software programs from logic charts, record layouts, and input and report formats.

7. Writes computer programs from logic flow charts, record layouts, and input and report formats.

8. Desk checks program for obvious errors and has it keypunched and compiled; creates JCL to test program, reviews output for correctness, and, if necessary, modifies program.

9. Assists computer operations personnel in implementing the productive running of jobs.

10. Formulates documentation for project, operations, and program in accordance with corporate and division standards.

11. Creates permanent files as required on disk storage device.

12. Assists the more-junior-level programmers in solving programming-related problems.

Organizational Relationships

Reports directly to the Project Leader, Systems. Has occasional contacts with managers or supervisors from various user departments to satisfy systems, program, or job flow requests. Has numerous contacts with Computer Operators and data conversion personnel to clarify data and procedures.

Position Specifications

Bachelor's Degree or equivalent required, plus 3–5 years experience in programming, some of which is in systems design. Working knowledge of accounting or manufacturing system, data management techniques, data communication concepts, and job control language. Must keep abreast of the latest techniques in the data processing industry, in particular when it affects programming and systems design.

TITLE OF POSITION: **Systems Analyst**

Basic Purpose

To develop and formulate the more complex and extensive computer data processing procedures having to do with business and/or mathematical problems. To provide technical information systems and services guidance to nontechnical user members of project task force.

Duties and Responsibilities

1. Represents the IS&S Department on task forces assigned to major systems projects, ensuring that systems development projects conform to corporate and division standards. Participates in conferences with potential and existing users of the facility to resolve problems relative to systems, formulas, computer procedure verification, need for data, and results desired.

2. Conducts interviews with user management and clerical personnel to determine specific requirements of new and revised systems as they affect their particular functions. Analyzes and evaluates proposed and existing systems in conjunction with the Manager, Information Systems and Services.

3. Reviews data prepared by Project Leaders and develops charts, tables, diagrams, and procedural statements illustrating data flow, formulas, and methods, with consideration for such factors as equipment capacities. Recommends modifications of basic systems detail to compensate for equipment limitations or

suggests where alteration may improve, simplify, or reduce operation costs.

4. Develops problem definitions, analyzes symptoms and problems, designs and proposes alternative solutions, and presents them for management decisions.

5. Prepares final statements, documents, and approved procedures for programming. May assist in the coding and/or debugging of computer programs and the initiation of advanced programming techniques.

6. Works closely with programming and computer operation personnel to guide and expedite work and resolve operational problems. Conducts hardware and software feasibility studies to support projects.

7. May perform as an alternate Project Leader on systems projects in order to ensure continuity of IS&S expertise.

8. Analyzes and evaluates computer test runs and prove-outs to determine if system is adequate and data meet needs.

9. Recommends procedural and programming logic to improve proficiency and accuracy in order to compensate for equipment limitations or failure and initiates such approved modifications.

10. Instructs and assists others engaged in programming and computer operations to train and otherwise orient personnel in department procedures.

11. Keeps informed of hardware and software product announcements and systems programming techniques for future application within the division.

12. Assists in training of user department personnel to enable them to fulfill their responsibilities in using computer-based systems.

Organizational Relationships

This position reports to the Project Leader, Manufacturing Systems. Position has extensive contact with all levels of user personnel and occasional contact with corporate IS&S counterparts. Frequent contact with hardware and software vendors. Provides technical expertise for major computer-based systems having potentially significant monetary impact within the division.

Position Specifications

Bachelor's Degree in Business Administration or equivalent plus 4–6 years experience in systems and procedures development, with enough experience in computer programming and processing to become familiar with computer theory and data application and to meet accuracy and proficiency requirements. Advanced courses in mathematics and electronic data processing logic beneficial.

TITLE OF POSITION: **Programmer**

Basic Purpose

To interpret systems, program, and job flow specifications developed by Project Leader, Systems in order to produce meaningful and efficient logic programs and operating techniques that will satisfy user requests.

Duties and Responsibilities

1. Reviews specifications and time estimates to determine if further clarification is required to produce results requested by user.

2. Creates computer program logic to process data to achieve meaningful output that will satisfy user request.

3. Prepares job control language (JCL) records to produce a logically sound job stream that could comprise one or more activities.

4. Develops data record layouts, input forms and record formats, proposed report formats, testing schemes, and test data.

5. Makes use of software programs or routines provided by computer manufacturer in areas of sort, utility, bulk media conversion, and so on.

6. Writes computer program from logic flow chart, record layouts, and input and report formats; spot checks program for obvious errors and has it keypunched and compiled; creates JCL to test program; and reviews output for correctness, and, if necessary, modifies program.

7. Assists computer operations personnel in implementing the productive running of the job.

8. Formulates documentation for project, operations, and program in accordance with corporate standards. Creates permanent files as required on disk storage device.

Organizational Relationships

This position reports to a Project Leader, Systems. May have day-to-day contact with computer operations and data conversion personnel.

Position Specifications

Bachelor's Degree or equivalent required, plus 1–3 years experience in programming. Working knowledge of accounting or manufacturing systems, data management techniques, data communication concepts, and job control language. Must keep abreast of the latest techniques in the data processing industry, particularly when it affects programming.

V

Engineering

TITLE OF POSITION: **Director, Product Engineering**

Basic Purpose

To plan, organize, and direct the Product Engineering Department to meet established objectives. To establish and maintain budgets and department procedures. To coordinate engineering activities with other departments in order to keep work schedules and increase efficiency.

Duties and Responsibilities

1. Provides direction to Engineering Department in the areas of design improvement, customer support, and production support and monitors programs to ensure that goals are met within budget and schedule limitations.

2. Ensures the maintenance of adequate records to support patent action; cooperates with patent counsel in obtaining patent protection for the company's unique processes and products.

3. Develops and recommends department objectives, plans, and budgets, consistent with division long- and short-range objectives.

4. Develops and maintains an effective organization through selection, evaluation, development, compensation, placement, and motivation of all product engineering personnel, and develops managerial talents and other talents necessary to achieve short- and long-range objectives by effective direction, counseling, and training according to an overall manpower plan.

5. Coordinates engineering activities with sales, manufacturing, material control, and other appropriate departments of the division.

6. Directs subordinates in the execution of their assigned responsibilities to ensure that their approach to meeting ob-

jectives and attaining satisfactory performance is consistent with established policies and procedures.

7. Prepares periodic reports and other data for presentation to Vice-President, Operations indicating record of achievement on established goals, recommended improvements, personnel requirements, expenses, and the like.

8. Confers with and assists staff personnel on day-to-day problems and procedures.

9. Directs the development of, and carrying out of, approved AAPs in accordance with the intent of Title VII of the Civil Rights Act of 1964.

10. Prepares and makes technical presentations to appropriate customer groups.

Organizational Relationships

This position reports to the Vice-President, Operations. Reporting directly to this position are three Managers of Product Engineering and one Secretary, and through them 40 professional Engineers, Designers, Checkers, and Draftspersons.

Position Specifications

Bachelor's Degree in Mechanical Engineering or equivalent education/work experience plus 12–14 years experience. Must have the ability to lead people, promote teamwork, and maintain a good rapport with customers.

TITLE OF POSITION: **Plant Engineer**

Basic Purpose

To plan, formulate, administer, and coordinate various engineering programs designed to improve plant operating performance and reduce waste and delays in the manufacturing process, and implement other, similar engineering programs to achieve better quality and lower costs. To evaluate, develop, and recommend improvements in manufacturing methods, layouts, and material handling equipment.

Duties and Responsibilities

1. Develops and maintains an effective organization through selection, development, compensation, and motivation of all engineering personnel. Develops managerial and other talents necessary to achieve short- and long-range objectives by efficient direction, counseling, and training according to an overall manpower plan.

2. Directs subordinates in the management of their assigned responsibilities to ensure that their responsibility to meet objectives and attain satisfactory operation and performance is consistent with established policies and procedures.

3. Prepares periodic reports or other data for presentation to Plant Manager indicating record of achievement on established goals, recommended improvements, personnel requirements, and the like.

4. Ensures the maintenance of various engineering records and prepares reports to measure the effectiveness of existing facilities and methods for current and projected manufacturing schedules. Ensures that staff proposals include factors such as efficiency, dependability, quality, and safety.

5. Manages and maintains a balanced organization possessing flexibility, maturity, and experience.

6. Recommends proper use of machines, tools, and equipment; appraises technological developments, investigating feasibility of new equipment and techniques; prepares dependable cost estimates for changes in manufacturing methods.

7. Directs the development of, and carrying out of, approved AAPs in the areas of EEOC compliance in accordance with the intent of Title VII of the Civil Rights Act of 1964.

8. Participates in development of new or improved products, recommends and specifies new materials and/or equipment, and designs the process flow.

9. May prepare manufacturing instruction as new products are approved for production; may oversee and advise on technical control over certain phases of production.

10. Periodically examines unit processes for updating techniques, quality, and overall efficiency.

11. Supervises the design and development of machinery equipment, jigs, and fixtures for production and quality assurance

test equipment. Recommends capital expenditures to Plant Manager.

12. May work closely with senior plant management and division employee relations in the development, evaluation, and placement of engineering personnel in related manufacturing departments.

13. Ensures compliance with applicable laws and regulations issued by OSHA, EPA, and other federal, state, and local regulatory agencies.

Organizational Relationships

This position reports to the Plant Manager. Reporting to this position are the Supervisor, Industrial Engineering; Engineer, Cost Estimating; Engineer, Industrial; Senior Clerk; Supervisor, Operations Support; and, through them, 16 clerical, 3 technical, and 22 professional employees.

Position Specifications

Graduate Industrial Engineer or equivalent education/work experience with 8–10 years progressive experience in a labor-intensive fabrication and assembly operation. Must have good planning ability, a strong analytical sense, and sound engineering approaches.

TITLE OF POSITION: **Project Engineer**

Basic Purpose

To serve as a technical adviser to location engineering personnel and Plant Managers, as assigned by the Vice-President, Operations, in their manufacturing projects and daily problem solving. To suggest and recommend solutions based on past experience and knowledge.

Duties and Responsibilities

1. Carries out special assignments and projects in broad areas upon request of the Vice-President, Operations; meets regu-

larly with Vice-President, Operations to review progress and to reestablish priorities.

2. Reviews and recommends approval of proposals as assigned, ensuring efficient production methods, flow of work, and use of space; follows completed projects to ensure that anticipated benefits are achieved.

3. Evaluates the effectiveness of facilities for projected manufacturing schedules, ensuring that dependable cost estimates are prepared to guide management in evaluating alternative proposals.

4. Participates in the development of long-range plans for major layout changes, incorporation of new processes, selection of equipment, and other related matters. Expedites certain segments of projects to avoid costly delays as assigned by the Vice-President, Operations.

5. Provides advice and counsel to the Purchasing Department in the preparation of materials and devices used in the product that reflect the highest quality, sufficient quantity, prompt delivery, and service required to meet production schedules.

6. Coordinates the fabrication and refinement of sample builds in conjunction with quality control prior to authorizing full production; reviews and recommends approval of manufacturing instructions as new products are released for production. Oversees various tests, inspections, trials, and production runs.

7. Evaluates unit processes for updating techniques, quality, and overall efficiency; may participate with plant engineers in designing special-purpose machinery and equipment for the product lines.

8. Institutes meaningful cost reduction programs as assigned at each plant location; recommends and specifies new materials and/or equipment when desirable.

Organizational Relationships

This position reports to the Vice-President, Operations. Regularly contacts customers, vendors, Plant Supervisers, Engineers, and Plant Managers. Other contacts are with buyers and production personnel.

Position Specifications
Bachelor's Degree in Industrial or Mechanical Engineering or equivalent education/work experience plus 10–12 years broad plant engineering and manufacturing experience.

TITLE OF POSITION: **Tooling Engineer**

Basic Purpose
To recommend tooling requirements for the injection molds used at all plant locations and to provide follow-up to ensure that appropriate tooling is purchased and used in accordance with division objectives. To ensure the timely completion of projects by vendors assigned by the division.

Duties and Responsibilities
1. Recommends the type and specification of new injection molds to produce parts for all locations. Utilizes a comprehensive knowledge of division products and their components and tooling operations, such as injection molds, insert molds, extruding plastics, blow molding, and fasteners of all types.

2. Maintains a constant awareness of the specialties and capabilities of a wide variety of firms supplying the required tooling. Recommends the selection of firms to supply the tooling required to produce plastic injection parts, blow molds, screw machine parts, and related components.

3. Reviews customer prints for new molds. Recommends changes in these designs to comply with product feasibility studies.

4. Makes timely investigations at various vendor locations to ensure conformance to required standards and time schedules. Recommends methods of resolving manufacturing problems as they arise.

5. Evaluates malfunctions of existing plastic molding tooling at the various locations and recommends corrective action.

6. Estimates the cost of engineering changes on tools assigned to this position and completes reports accordingly.

7. Maintains status on all affected tooling projects and provides this information to appropriate personnel. Informs immediate superior of all problems in assigned area of responsibility.

8. Provides layout group with new parts from new tooling with all required information, such as print level, number of cavities, and schedule for completion. Evaluates completed layout reports with product engineering and determines corrective action when necessary.

9. Performs a variety of special manufacturing assignments at plant locations involving efficiency analysis, methods engineering, tooling repair, and other problem-solving functions.

Organizational Relationships

Reports directly to the Manager, Tool Engineering. Has numerous inside contacts with purchasing, product engineering, and production personnel for the interpretation and interchange of information. Has numerous outside contacts with vendors for the above purposes.

Position Specifications

Bachelor's Degree in Mechanical Engineering or the equivalent plus 4–6 years of practical experience in manufacturing and tool engineering. Must have comprehensive knowledge of division products and tools for plastic molds.

TITLE OF POSITION: **Mechanical Engineer**

Basic Purpose

To plan, coordinate, and control all engineering activities associated with operation methods, process, time standards, tooling, material routing, preparation of estimates, and other technical phases involved in the production of company products.

Duties and Responsibilities

1. Researches and implements advanced technology in the area of tooling, mechanization, and automation to reduce cost of manufacture.

2. Conducts continuous study projects on existing manufacturing standards to effect cost reductions through the use of advanced engineering concepts and manufacturing innovations.

3. Works closely with division tool engineering, product engineering, and manufacturing personnel to plan operations, resolve problems, evaluate new methods and tool designs, and carry out related matters.

4. Prepares cost estimates for manufacturing and new tooling, using standard application data where possible and developing original data as required.

5. Analyzes and investigates cost of manufacturing reports to detect areas of excessive expenditures, determine causes, and recommend and effect corrective procedures.

6. Oversees the documentation of standard applications for records and files.

7. Prepares periodic or special reports having to do with manufacturing costs, causes of variances, machine and tooling cost data, anticipated cost reductions and savings, and related matters for management information and analysis.

8. Appraises employee performances and recommends changes of status and salary adjustments within limitations of company policy.

9. Determines, documents, and maintains appropriate routing sheets, equipment lists, spare parts, inventory, and layouts for the manufacturing operation.

10. Designs and develops specifications on tools, fixtures, and equipment for manufacturing processes.

11. Provides vendor contact/surveillance for tools, fixtures, and equipment to determine cost effectiveness of proposed product and process improvement.

12. Designs safeguards for equipment and processes.

13. Advises maintenance personnel engaged in setups of welders, riveters, pneumatic fixtures, epoxy dispensers, inspection gauges, and marking equipment.

14. Plans and conducts investigative studies on excessive

production costs and initiates, implements, and guides cost reduction programs to favorable conclusion.

15. Provides assistance to the Plant Manager on major projects such as expansion of facilities, acquisition and installation of capital equipment, major repairs and overhauls, plant layout changes, and other related matters to the best economic advantage and schedule.

16. Organizes and develops comprehensive cost estimates for various plant applications. Evaluates and analyzes the design of each application to determine the most economical and functional systems, methods, and procedures for manufacture and appropriate tools, equipment, and facilities.

Organizational Relationships

This position reports to the Plant Manager. Coordinates work activities with maintenance, production, quality assurance, and purchasing personnel.

Position Specifications

Bachelor's Degree in Mechanical or Industrial Engineering or equivalent education/work experience plus 8–10 years manufacturing experience. Must have a comprehensive knowledge of pneumatic schematics, welding, and assembly techniques, and design experience.

TITLE OF POSITION: **Cost-Estimating Engineer**

Basic Purpose

To conduct complex and involved value and cost analysis engineering studies in order to determine standard manufacturing costs and means of effecting cost reduction through improving manufacturing specifications, changing product designs, and other related facets affecting product cost.

103

Duties and Responsibilities

1. Evaluates existing and proposed product designs of company products, in accordance with sound engineering principles, to determine manufacturing cost estimates.

2. Compiles and audits product cost as to materials and manufacturing, breaking out components and operations for purposes of detailed cost analysis.

3. Evaluates product cost items and prepares recommendations to effect cost reductions in materials, tooling, labor, design configuration, and related items.

4. Confers and coordinates procedures with manufacturing and engineering personnel to obtain and impart information and research and verify data involved in analyses.

5. Conducts investigative studies in areas of excessive costs to determine cause and initiate corrective measures. Provides detailed evaluations and proposals regarding solutions to complex problems.

6. Follows and coordinates engineering changes in the areas of purchasing, marketing, and sales where provisions affect product cost.

7. Coordinates department administration procedures having to do with systems records and files.

8. Prepares and provides a wide variety of reports for management information and decision making, including such reports as break-even analysis and cost of sales versus cost of manufacture.

9. Serves as technical expert for department personnel regarding all areas of cost estimating and related implications.

Organizational Relationships

This position reports to the Manager, Engineering Services. Has frequent contacts with personnel from all levels of management for the analysis and interchange of technical information.

Position Specifications

Bachelor's Degree in Engineering or the equivalent plus 6–8 years experience in various engineering fields, such as production, tooling, and manufacturing, to acquire the broad technical background needed to carry out assignments.

TITLE OF POSITION: **Manufacturing Engineer**

Basic Purpose

To organize, manage, and participate in the development of industrial and manufacturing engineering and cost estimates for product, facilities, equipment, and staffing levels. To interpret, explain, and justify cost estimates to top management personnel.

Duties and Responsibilities

1. Organizes and develops comprehensive cost estimates for company products. Evaluates and analyzes the design of each part to determine the most economical methods and procedures for manufacture and defines appropriate tools, equipment, and facilities.

2. Determines and documents appropriate routing sheets, equipment lists, manning charts, skill level requirements, and plant layouts. Evaluates and analyzes products to determine facility costs and associated fixed and variable costs such as taxes, depreciation, and the like. Consults with outside organizations and other sources to estimate and compile these costs.

3. Presents this comprehensive cost information to top management of division for evaluation. Interprets and justifies details of costs as required. Makes various adjustments to portions of cost estimate package in accordance with directions from management.

4. Prepares requisitions for equipment, tools, new facilities, refurbishment of existing facilities, utilities, and raw materials for new product systems.

5. Coordinates various adjustments such as engineering changes and related deviations with vendors as required.

6. Prepares comprehensive layout schedules and flow charts, including such information as hiring schedules, delivery schedules, lead times, cash payment requirements, cost information, target production dates, start-up dates, and related information and presents to appropriate product manager. Attaches tooling lists, manning charts, summary of skill levels, and related schedules as required.

7. Performs functions such as instructing and demonstrating new equipment to employees; documenting and setting up welding schedules; supervising all phases of plant layout; performs related industrial engineering functions, such as motion study and the study of methods, sequences, and related applications; and other key start-up activities. Debugs new systems until they are totally operational.

8. Conceptualizes designs of test equipment and processes related to new products and provides to tool and equipment design group for subsequent action.

9. Evaluates and analyzes costs and techniques of new concepts, disciplines, or applications for manufacturing processes, such as the use of automatic screw machines, chemical machining, and other applications. Presents relevant data to upper management for further evaluation.

10. Develops, supervises, and maintains assigned staff in order to attain the required objectives. Compensates, motivates, and disciplines subordinates in accordance with division policies and procedures. Conducts merit reviews on a timely basis.

11. Carries out approved affirmative action plans in the areas of Equal Employment Opportunity Commission compliance in accordance with the intent of Title VII of the Civil Rights Act of 1964.

Organizational Relationships

Reports directly to Manager, Advanced Manufacturing Planning. Continually interrelates with product engineering, quality assurance, and purchasing regarding the coordination of technical information. Interfaces with Controller's department for the interchange of information. Position has numerous outside contacts with engineering firms and a wide variety of vendors for the coordination of technical information. Position also has occasional contacts with corporation departments regarding environmental impact and equipment selection for chemical processing operations.

Position Specifications

Incumbent must have a Bachelor's Degree in Industrial Engineering or the equivalent plus 6–8 years related experience.

Must have a comprehensive knowledge of equipment and tooling, metal cutting and finishing procedures, stamping, plating, heat treating, molding, and the characteristics of metal, plastics, textiles, and electronic components.

TITLE OF POSITION: **Production Engineer**

Basic Purpose

To plan, manage, and coordinate production engineering functions for the purpose of providing technical support and controlling product design and documentation required to produce quality products at minimum cost.

Duties and Responsibilities

1. Confers with the Director, Product Engineering on technical matters pertinent to long-range planning of the production support groups and resolution of design-related production problems. Ensures that policies, procedures, control systems, and technical direction of the Director, Product Engineering are implemented and followed.

2. Establishes and implements a program for the review of all scrap and rejected parts for possible rework.

3. Provides support to vendors in resolving technical problems and improving the quality of supplied parts.

4. Oversees the added efforts of engineers in evaluating and determining reasons for assembly and test failure problems. Recommends appropriate action to other location department heads to resolve such problems.

5. Supervises the review and approval of customer drawings as well as revised and/or new internal drawings prior to production release, first article layout reports, gauge designs, and finished gauges. Recommends approval of material purchase orders.

6. Cooperates with quality control to establish and implement set-up procedures for the layout of parts; determines the appropriate dimensions of parts to be checked; and initiates,

coordinates, and monitors test programs and evaluates results relative to performance and reliability.

7. Participates in the conception, evaluation, and implementation of cost reduction, product improvement, and production problem-solving activities.

8. Obtains approvals on desired optional changes and internally requested changes, effective date on changes, customer-requested deviations, and related adjustments from the Sales Department.

9. Oversees the evaluation and establishment of "quick fixes" to solve shutdown or very high reject-type problems.

10. Maintains appropriate files of engineering drawings, history drawings, reference drawings, engineering records, specifications, deviation forms, material and inventory records, and related information.

11. Evaluates and approves or rejects all internally requested engineering changes and deviations. Coordinates department activities with plant departments to collect information and approvals required on internally requested engineering changes prior to submission to the Sales Department. Interfaces with the customer as required to obtain approvals on such changes.

12. Maintains a thorough knowledge of, and provides technical guidance to all departments on, federal regulations and customer specifications relative to company products.

13. Maintains a local engineering cost control system and deviation reporting program. Oversees the preparation and distribution of reports documenting engineering studies, directions, and programs.

14. Participates in a wide variety of engineering activities, including the processing and follow-up on distribution of prints and specifications, the creation of charts and assembly and subassembly drawings, various design studies and related reports, the processing of new releases and engineering changes, the evaluation of the recommendation on optional changes, the notification of approved deviations, the preparation and maintenance of material and inventory files, and the creation of control sheets.

15. Provides technical support to plant departments on customer-requested prototype build programs.

Organizational Relationships

This position reports administratively to the Plant Manager and is directed on engineering policy, procedures, and technical matters by the Director, Product Engineering. Continually inter-relates with quality control, material control, tooling, purchasing, manufacturing, development engineering, and sales on technical matters.

Position Specifications

Bachelor's Degree in Engineering or equivalent plus 8–10 years experience in engineering, including experience in a super-visory capacity. Must be capable of using discretion in dealing with others and of organizing and motivating others.

VI

Manufacturing and Maintenance

TITLE OF POSITION: **Vice-President, Operations**

Basic Purpose

To develop plans and strategies for the direction and administration of the division's business activities, including materials management, tool engineering, sales and liaison engineering, cost estimating, manufacturing, product engineering, and technical service, to attain objectives based on corporate and division goals and policies.

Duties and Responsibilities

1. Directs and administers the division's business activities, including materials management, tool engineering, sales and liaison engineering, cost estimating, manufacturing, product engineering, and technical service, to attain objectives based on corporate and division goals and policies.

2. Directs development of business plans and strategies consistent with short- and long-range objectives of the division and corporation.

3. Directs immediate subordinates in the management of their assigned areas to ensure that their responsibilities to attain objectives and satisfactory operation and performance are met in a way that is consistent with established policies and programs.

4. Analyzes and appraises, regularly and systematically, the effectiveness of all operations to ensure that established objectives will be met, that corporate and division policies will be observed, and that prompt corrective action will be taken when necessary.

5. Develops and maintains an effective organization through the selection, training, compensation, and motivation of all personnel.

111

6. Develops management talents necessary to obtain short- and long-range goals by effective direction, counseling, and training according to an overall manpower plan. Approves or recommends approval of organization structure and manning requirements.

7. Maintains the necessary communication and coordination with Vice-President and Controller; Vice-President, Product Assurance; Vice-President, Technical Services; and pertinent officials of corporate offices and other divisions.

8. Reviews and evaluates contracts and appropriations and expenditure requests submitted by immediate subordinates, approving those within authority and submitting those above authority to the division President with recommendations.

9. Determines and establishes, through joint consideration and planning, long- and short-term manufacturing objectives consistent with existing sales, projected sales forecasts, inventory requirements, and other factors involved.

10. Reviews reports on manufacturing activities, performance, and results and initiates action to correct deviations and variables as to schedules, excessive costs, material shortages, or other deterrent factors.

11. Recommends changes in existing policies necessary to the improved conduct of the business for the approval of the President or other higher levels of management.

12. Provides the most reliable projections of future performance that can be developed, as well as reliable reports of current performance. Ensures that this information is communicated to the President and to those responsible for management reporting of long- and/or short-range planning.

13. Ensures that all assigned departments meet objectives and conform to the policies and procedures of the company.

14. Directs the development of and carrying out of approved affirmative action programs in the areas of EEOC compliance in accordance with the intent of Title VII of the Civil Rights Act of 1964.

15. Ensures compliance with applicable laws and regulations issued by OSHA, EPA, and other federal, state, and local regulatory agencies.

112

Organizational Relationships

This position reports directly to the President. Reporting to this position are Plant Managers; Director, Materials; Director, Product Engineering; Director, Sales; Manager, Tool Engineering; and a Senior Engineer, Project. Coordinates activities with division Directors and Vice-Presidents.

Position Specifications

Prefer Bachelor's Degree in Engineering or equivalent work experience, plus 15–18 years of diversified overall related business experience, including Director-level experience. Should possess characteristics indicating ability to exercise sound judgment and leadership in making management decisions. Excellent verbal and written communication skills required.

TITLE OF POSITION: **Plant Manager**

Basic Purpose

To plan, direct, and coordinate all plant operations in accordance with preestablished company and division production objectives at optimum cost consistent with quality requirements.

Duties and Responsibilities

1. Develops and maintains an effective organization through selection, training, compensation, and motivation of all personnel. Develops management talents necessary to obtain short- and long-range goals by effective direction, counseling, and training. Develops organization structures and manning requirements.

2. Directs maintenance or physical condition of all facilities, either through a systematic program of repairs or through initiation of fixed capital requests when this action appears economic or appropriate.

3. Monitors operating conditions and manufacturing schedules on a frequent basis and through frequent contacts with division Manufacturing, Sales, and Materials Departments and

suggests more desirable conditions or levels of operations to meet inventory or sales demands.

4. Initiates various programs that lead to improved quality, decreased effluent pollutions, lower costs, and overall efficiency.

5. Directs those activities that provide assurance that safety, health, and environmental rules and regulations are met or exceeded.

6. Manages administration of labor contracts; seeks assistance of Vice-President, Operations and Employee Relations Department in resolving difficult contract interpretations and guidance in preparing for arbitration cases.

7. Directs the preparation of budgets and provides regular and special expense and cost control reports, requesting assistance from the Controller's department when required.

8. Develops and maintains good relations with neighbors and communities surrounding the location by encouraging personnel to participate in community affairs and activities and to establish frequent contacts with community leaders. Sets the general tenor of company relationship with the community, and maintains personal contacts with local officials in influential positions.

9. Directs the various department Managers in the preparation and implementation of plant operating plans and strategies consistent with the agreed-to business plan. Guides the Manager in the preparation of annual budget goals. Forecasts and advises the Managers of deviations from the plan with advance notice so that corrective action can be taken.

10. Determines plant policies consistent with division and corporate policies, and directs and supervises the application of such policies to the plant's manufacturing operations.

11. Develops improved manufacturing methods, layouts, equipment, and techniques and submits recommendations for approval. Conducts a continuous cost reduction program through the plant.

12. Provides expertise to the line organization in the development of standards of performance in all areas of product responsibility. Administers expenditure of funds to carry on plant operations.

13. Ensures compliance with applicable laws and regula-

tions issued by OSHA, EPA, and federal, state, and local regulatory agencies.

14. Directs the development of, and carrying out of, approved AAPs in the areas of EEOC compliance in accordance with the intent of Title VII of the Civil Rights Act of 1964.

Organizational Relationships

This position reports to the Vice-President, Operations. Reporting to this position are Managers of Production and Maintenance, Employee Relations, Product Engineering, Industrial Engineering, Environmental Services, Quality Assurance, and Materials Control, and the Plant Controller.

Position Specifications

Bachelor's Degree in Industrial or Mechanical Engineering or equivalent plus 10–12 years broad engineering and manufacturing experience, including supervisory experience, in a labor-intensive fabrication/assembly or related operation.

TITLE OF POSITION: **Manager, Operations**

Basic Purpose

To manage and coordinate all areas of production, maintenance, and related services through Managers/Superintendents to achieve timely production of quality parts at the most economical costs and in the proper quantities. To maintain and develop both a safe facility environment and a workforce capable of meeting manufacturing and maintenance requirements in the present and future to attain objectives in accordance with production and delivery schedules.

Duties and Responsibilities

1. Manages and organizes maintenance operations to utilize skills and experience of the maintenance workforce to the best advantage, to obtain the most favorable repair costs and quality of

115

workmanship, and to prevent interruption of production schedules; ensures the development of a maintenance engineering program designed to establish maintenance material standards and specifications, lubrication requirements, standard maintenance procedures, and maintenance methods studies/improvements; evaluates existing and proposed facilities to improve operating and maintenance efficiency or to ensure economical design and construction.

2. Plans the use of facilities, equipment, and personnel to meet current and future manufacturing requirements, including department budgets and guidelines, plant layout and improvements, and capital expenditure programs.

3. Acts as the liaison between management and the workforce to keep plant production and maintenance supervision informed, avoid breach of contract, and maintain the highest possible level of employee/employer relationships.

4. Develops and recommends approval of an operating budget for each section supervised and initiates action to operate within those fiscal plans.

5. Maintains uninterrupted production and product quality and quantity within the limitations of established manufacturing costs and budget allocations.

6. Recommends, expedites, implements, and coordinates approved procedures having to do with utilizing staff services to resolve manufacturing problems and difficulties.

7. Manages production operation to ensure scheduled work flow and use of personnel, skills, machines, and facilities and directs and expedites machine repairs and correction of other problems obstructing production procedures.

8. Uses motivating techniques and delegates responsibilities and appropriate authority to subordinate supervisory and staff personnel to achieve maximum efficiency through proper use of skills, man-hours, machines, and equipment.

9. Supervises inventories of machine replacement parts, materials, and supplies to ensure that they are maintained at proper levels.

10. Manages a program of preventive maintenance and die repair in accordance with production needs and division regulations and objectives.

11. Ensures the use of proper safety devices, equipment, and methods and maintenance of general housekeeping; maintains a constant awareness of and takes corrective action on hazardous conditions and practices.

12. Participates in plant management meetings to assist in planning and to make recommendations on matters related to manufacturing and maintenance operations.

13. Implements general administrative and technical programs, such as communications, staffing, employee training, employee relations, grievances, disciplinary actions, and cost reductions.

14. Manages and maintains a proper plant maintenance and manufacturing workforce.

15. Develops, supervises, and maintains own department in order to attain the required objectives. Compensates, motivates, and disciplines subordinates in accordance with current division policies and procedures.

16. Conducts and ensures the conduct of merit reviews on a timely basis.

17. Carries out approved affirmative action plans in the areas of Equal Employment Opportunity Commission compliance in accordance with the intent of Title VII of the Civil Rights Act of 1964.

18. Ensures compliance with applicable laws and regulations issued by OSHA, EPA, and other federal, state, and local regulatory agencies.

19. Implements and controls a management by objectives program for own department.

20. Manages own department in the appropriate manner to provide optimum union relations in accordance with union contract. Provides accurate feedback by appropriate management personnel regarding potential union/labor problems and possible solutions. Serves as manufacturing representative during union contract negotiations.

Organizational Relationships

Reports directly to the Plant Manager. Directly supervises the Manager, Metal Fabrication and Manager, Facilities and Maintenance. Frequent contact with other plant department heads and division managerial personnel and with other plant locations.

Position Specifications

Bachelor's Degree in Industrial Management or Industrial Engineering or related discipline plus a good knowledge of related areas to acquire sufficient background as to procedures, skill, and supervisory techniques and to accomplish the basic position purpose. Eight to ten years of related manufacturing experience, preferably including experience as a Plant Superintendent/ Manager.

TITLE OF POSITION: **Manager, Facilities and Electrical Engineering**

Basic Purpose

To plan and coordinate activities involved in the maintenance and alteration of facilities and equipment, including the movement, installation, repair, and overhaul of machines, tools, and plant equipment. To supervise and coordinate the electrical engineering section in the machining, fabrication, and construction of pilot models and the mechanical and electrical testing of component parts.

Duties and Responsibilities

1. Formulates and implements an effective preventive maintenance program.

2. Supervises and expedites emergency repairs necessary to minimize costly downtime and to maintain production schedules. Researches, plans, and prepares proposals for approval relative to procurement of capital equipment, expansion, construction, major maintenance projects, service contracts, and other related matters.

3. Supervises inventories of machine replacement parts,

materials, and supplies to see that they are maintained at proper levels.

4. Instructs and assists personnel and inspects work to ensure compliance with customer and engineering specifications as to dimensions, tolerances, and materials used in company products.

5. Checks test setups and devices and test specifications, procedures, and sequences to assure conformance to directives.

6. Provides assistance to the Plant Manager on major projects such as expansion of facilities, acquisition and installation of capital equipment, major repairs and overhauls, plant layout changes, and other related matters to the best economic advantage and schedule.

7. Resolves problems that develop during test runs, makes recommendations, and renders technical engineering assistance on test defects and deviations.

8. Analyzes engineering designs as to dimensions, material specifications, mechanics, and other engineering factors to standardize components, units, materials, and designs where feasible in accordance with model, application, capacity, and dimension to effect simplification of designs, interchangeable parts, and reduction of inventories and manufacturing costs.

9. Adheres to and assists in monitoring spirit of the corporation's EEO philosophy.

10. Ensures compliance with applicable laws and regulations issued by OSHA, EPA, and other federal agencies.

Organizational Relationships

This position reports to the Plant Manager. Coordinates activities with customers and vendors for all equipment and standards.

Position Specifications

Bachelor's Degree in Electrical Engineering or equivalent education/work experience, plus 8–10 years experience in electronics and maintenance.

TITLE OF POSITION: **Supervisor, Maintenance**

Basic Purpose

To supervise the maintenance activity through the implementation of a preventive maintenance program and an ongoing maintenance repair program for the facility, vehicles, production maintenance, and process equipment.

Duties and Responsibilities

1. Plans and implements effective procedures and policies for the maintenance department to ensure that all equipment, facilities, and utilities are in an acceptable state of repair.

2. Coordinates with vendors, suppliers, and contractors the installation of new equipment or equipment processes.

3. Establishes, with direction from the Plant Manager, priorities of all maintenance activities through a work order procedure.

4. Supervises all daily activities of the Maintenance Department through subordinates to ensure completion of assigned projects that will result in the least amount of machine downtime.

5. Monitors completion of maintenance projects to ensure that safety and quality standards are met.

6. Approves all requisitions relating to new and replacement parts, supplies, machinery, and equipment for the Maintenance Department.

7. Provides technical knowledge and expertise to solve problems of a mechanical, electrical, or hydraulic/pneumatic nature.

8. Develops and maintains responsible labor/management relations consistent with the labor agreement, including representing the company in certain grievances.

9. Schedules and assigns hourly personnel to maintain good housekeeping for the facility grounds and administrative offices.

Organizational Relationships

This position reports to the Manager, Engineering and Maintenance and indirectly to the Plant Manager. Reporting to this position are two foremen and up to ten hourly employees. Coordinates work with all service and production departments.

120

Position Specifications

Must possess Master Electrician's License plus 8–10 years experience in maintenance, engineering, or related fields. Prefer minimum of 3–5 years supervisory experience. Must be familiar with each of the following areas: boilers, air compressors, heating and air conditioning, plumbing, welding, carpentry, electrical/ electronic equipment, pneumatic hydraulics, and heavy manufacturing equipment.

TITLE OF POSITION: **General Foreman, Electrical Assembly**

Basic Purpose

To supervise the production and manufacture of company products, satisfying all reliability and quality standards mandated by customers and government specifications in the most effective and economical manner possible.

Duties and Responsibilities

1. Plans, organizes, and controls assigned manufacturing operations in accordance with guidelines and schedules established by the Plant Manager.

2. Maintains total awareness of division and plant policies, regulations, and procedures, and ensures proper adherence to them with respect to all electrical assembly operations.

3. Develops, trains, and motivates hourly employees through subordinates to acquire maximum efficiency, productivity, cooperation, and morale.

4. Maintains close surveillance over assembly operations to ensure scheduled work and material flow; proper use of manpower, skills, equipment, and facilities; proper application of methods; and related matters.

5. Provides instructions, guidance, and directions to assist foremen having assembly difficulties and procedural problems.

6. Coordinates and participates in general administrative and technical programs such as cost reduction, methods, communications, safety and housekeeping, and employee training.

121

7. Participates in employee relations procedures as directed and as stated contractually.

8. Interacts with staff support groups to expedite any changes in department operations and works with other supervisory personnel to meet production schedules and to assist in meeting cost reduction and quality improvement objectives.

9. Anticipates production problems such as potential delays, material shortages, equipment repairs, and the like, and devises and implements procedures to prevent or minimize loss of man-hours and scheduled interruptions.

10. Ensures proper disposition of rework and scrap through repair of such items or documentation of material that is scrapped.

11. Identifies employees for consideration for promotion to help meet objectives of the affirmative action plan; takes necessary action to prevent or stop harassment of employees.

Organizational Relationships

This position reports to the Plant Manager. Position interacts with other staff activities, such as employee relations, accounting, and materials management.

Position Specifications

High school graduate with 7–10 years manufacturing experience, including 3–4 years experience at the foreman level. Must have knowledge of various techniques, tooling, electronic equipment, and quality control procedures.

TITLE OF POSITION: **Foreman, Electrical Assembly**

Basic Purpose

To supervise hourly personnel directly during production start-up and manufacture of company products, satisfying all reliability and quality standards mandated by the customer in the most economical manner possible.

Duties and Responsibilities

1. Plans, organizes, and controls shift operations in accordance with guidelines established by production schedules and the General Foreman. Maintains total awareness of policies, regulations, and procedures, and ensures compliance by all assigned employees.

2. Develops, trains, and motivates hourly employees to acquire maximum efficiency, productivity, cooperation, and morale.

3. Ensures that all shift employees, equipment, materials, and areas of operation conform to all appropriate health and safety regulations.

4. Conducts safety meetings, at least monthly, to ensure that safe practices and conduct are maintained at all times.

5. Rewards and disciplines shift employees in accordance with established policies and the local labor agreement. Maintains full documentation for all actions taken.

6. Refers shift employees to appropriate support department in order to resolve various problems, including, but not limited to, insurance coverage, pension information, interpretation of policy, and other work-related subjects that cannot be answered by the incumbent.

7. Ensures that assigned area of responsibility is maintained with good housekeeping practices.

8. Schedules vacations for hourly personnel in accordance with individual requests, division policy, local labor agreements, and production schedules.

Organizational Relationships

This position reports to the General Foreman, Electrical Assembly. Reporting to this position are up to 30 hourly employees. This position interacts with staff activities such as material/production control and employee relations.

Position Specifications

High school graduate plus 7–10 years manufacturing experience. Must possess the ability to organize and to direct and motivate people and have potential for further advancement. Must have knowledge of electronic, quality control, and assembly techniques, equipment, tooling, and processes.

VII

Marketing and Sales

TITLE OF POSITION: **Director, Marketing and Sales**

Basic Purpose

To plan, direct, and control various technical service activities that satisfy customer requirements in the areas of purchasing, engineering, and quality control. To direct the formulation and implementation of sales plans and marketing strategies that support company profit objectives. To plan, coordinate, and recommend to senior management various promotion and sales strategies of new products to achieve maximum market penetration and pricing consistent with short- and long-term objectives.

Duties and Responsibilities

1. Develops and maintains an effective organization through selection, development, compensation, and motivation of all personnel; develops managerial and other talents necessary to achieve short- and long-range objectives by effective direction, counseling, and training according to an overall manpower plan.

2. Develops and recommends specific sales and marketing objectives and forecasts for products sold; directs the execution of authorized sales plans and marketing programs to achieve or exceed profit volume and other sales and marketing objectives.

3. Develops and recommends pricing strategy based on evaluation of economic conditions, competition, and state and federal legislation that affects the marketability of company products. Participates in negotiations on product pricing agreements.

4. Maintains favorable relations with all customers, including directing the administration of all promotional activities, and ensures that all customer entertainment is in line with corporate policy and procedures.

5. Evaluates and recommends new product development and sales to appropriate senior management.

6. Evaluates customer requests for product modification or improvement, recommending action to engineering group.

7. Reviews major complaints received from customers for the purpose of defining the actual problem, resolving the complaint, and determining where emphasis should be placed to prevent recurrence.

8. Advises division management and manufacturing facilities of quality problems, ensuring that corrective action is taken and that customers are properly notified.

9. Maintains regular communications with necessary departments for the purpose of scheduling new tooling programs, engineering changes, and quality standards.

10. Visits customers on a regular basis with department staff to maintain sound customer relations.

11. Keeps division management informed of competitors' activities through preview of information from internal and external sources.

12. Directs immediate subordinates in the management of their assigned responsibilities to ensure that their responsibility to attain objectives and satisfactory operations and performance is met in a way that is consistent with established policies and programs.

13. Manages and maintains a balanced organization possessing the necessary flexibility, technical skills, and experience to support short- and long-range requirements effectively.

14. Ensures development and implementation of an affirmative action plan in accordance with EEO regulations.

15. Ensures compliance with applicable laws and regulations and product quality standards issued by OSHA, EPA, and other federal, state, and local regulatory agencies.

Organizational Relationships

This position reports directly to the Vice-President, Operations. Reporting to this position are two Sales Managers; one Manager, Cost Control; and one Supervisor, Contract Compliance. Position interfaces daily with manufacturing services, quality control, and engineering. Maintains regular contact with customers.

Position Specifications

Bachelor's Degree in Marketing or Mechanical Engineering with 12–14 years related experience, including experience as a Manager, Marketing and Sales. Must possess a high level of maturity and exercise sound judgment in all dealings and associations with customers.

TITLE OF POSITION: **Manager, Sales**

Basic Purpose

To plan, coordinate, and manage all sales and technical service activities related to the various company products from initial design to maintenance of approved programs.

Duties and Responsibilities

1. Reviews and discusses, internally, proposed engineering drawings submitted by customers on future programs to determine feasibility from a manufacturing standpoint, and ultimately approves or rejects said drawings.

2. Coordinates all sales and marketing activities to recommend an acceptable selling price and authorizes submission of price quotations to customers. Releases and authorizes tooling for approved customer final designs to tool engineering groups. Meets with, and reviews production requirements of new programs with, division and location manufacturing groups.

3. Releases new colors of products sold and component parts to material control, purchasing, and quality control and obtains samples from each for submission to and final approval by each customer.

4. Accepts customers' pilot build requirements, conveys required information to purchasing, tool engineering, manufacturing engineering, and quality personnel at each plant location, and ensures that various delivery dates are met.

5. Ensures that all company products meet federal and state specifications through independent laboratory approval.

6. Develops and recommends specific sales and marketing objectives and forecasts for products sold; manages the execution of authorized sales plans and marketing programs to achieve or exceed profit volume and other sales and marketing objectives.

7. Establishes target dates and coordinates internal activities to ensure that first article production and facility approval will be obtained from the customer.

8. Ensures that proper flow of required information on all programs and program changes is distributed to each operating element of the organization.

9. Coordinates the overall establishment of selling prices, tooling bills, and cost of engineering changes.

10. Advises manufacturing facilities of quality problems, ensuring that corrective action is taken and that customers are properly notified.

11. Participates in various presentations to customers on product improvements, price increases, new product programs, and other related matters.

12. Visits customers on a regular basis with department staff to maintain sound customer relations.

13. Manages and maintains a balanced organization possessing flexibility, technical skills, and long-range requirements. Develops and maintains a professional staff through selection, development, compensation, and motivation.

14. Directs immediate subordinates in the management of their assigned responsibilities to ensure that their responsibility to attain objectives and satisfactory operation and performance is met in a way that is consistent with established policies and programs.

15. Manages the administration of assigned promotional sales activities and ensures that all customer entertainment is in line with corporate policy and procedures.

16. Directs the performance of and carrying out of appropriate AAPs in the areas of EEOC compliance in accordance with the intent of Title VII of the Civil Rights Act of 1964.

Organizational Relationships

This position reports to the Director, Marketing and Sales. Reporting to this position are three Liaison Engineers and related clerical support. Interfaces daily with manufacturing departments, quality assurance, and engineering. Maintains regular contact with each customer.

Position Specifications

Bachelor's Degree in Mechanical Engineering or Marketing or equivalent education/work experience with a minimum of 8–10 years related experience. Incumbent must possess a high level of maturity and exercise sound judgment in all dealings and associations with customers.

TITLE OF POSITION: **Manager, Cost Control**

Basic Purpose

To establish the criteria for, guide, manage, and control product manufacturing cost and selling prices in order to obtain minimum product cost and optimum product revenue.

Duties and Responsibilities

1. Manages the evaluation of product engineering change requests and advises the organization of the cost and price effect of these changes.

2. Evaluates the effect of product cost changes related to process revisions or economic conditions and furnishes this information to the organization.

3. Manages the establishment of manufacturing requirements and operating standards used in the development of product costing and pricing.

4. Controls and coordinates the development of all manufacturing process routings.

5. Provides guidance and direction to the manufacturing location industrial engineering organizations related to the impact of method or process change on their actions.

6. Reviews and recommends approval of all requests for revisions to manufacturing, quantitative requirements, methods, and operating standards.

7. Conducts periodic audits of the manufacturing locations' actual processes, comparing product cost to planned standard cost.

8. Conducts price negotiations with customer cost analysis groups and customer purchasing departments.

9. Manages and controls the development of cost and price for all billable and nonbillable tooling programs.

10. Provides substantiation and negotiates settlements for all customer audit requirements pertaining to tooling changes and cancellation claims.

11. Provides guidance regarding timely and accurate receipt and shipping of customer orders.

12. Furnishes projected schedules of short- and long-range customer demands to the organization.

13. Establishes the authorized finished product inventory levels for the manufacturing locations.

14. Develops and maintains an effective organization through selection, development, compensation, and motivation of all assigned personnel; develops managerial and other talents necessary to achieve short- and long-range objectives by effective direction, counseling, and training according to an overall manpower plan.

15. Manages the development of, and carrying out of, approved AAPs in the areas of EEOC compliance in accordance with the intent of Title VII of the Civil Rights Act of 1964.

Organizational Relationships

This position reports to the Director, Marketing and Sales. Interfaces daily with accounting, product engineering, and industrial engineering. Maintains a close contact with plant operations. Directly supervises one Supervisor, Cost Estimating; two Cost Engineers; one Supervisor, Administrative Services; and two Supervisors, Customer Contact.

Position Specifications

Bachelor's Degree, preferably in Industrial or Mechanical Engineering, Accounting, or Marketing or equivalent education/

work experience plus 8–10 years related experience, including supervisory experience. Must possess a high level of maturity and tact and be capable of exercising sound judgment.

TITLE OF POSITION: **Supervisor, Contract Compliance**

Basic Purpose

To provide and interpret highly technical data on all company products and systems built by the company to appropriate federal and state agencies and obtain approvals for manufacture as necessary. To maintain the status on approval applications as required.

Duties and Responsibilities

1. Provides hardware and a wide variety of technical data regarding specifications of components, parts, and assemblies of products to appropriate federal and state agencies. Interprets aspects of this information from multiview drawings, material specifications, torque specifications, and related sources for the benefit of agency personnel. Obtains the necessary approvals for the subsequent manufacture and distribution of these products or systems after federal and state testing.

2. Analyzes all physical changes resulting from corrective actions to ensure subsequent compliance with federal and/or state regulations after implementation.

3. Analyzes and evaluates technical data from federal and state sample failures. Makes recommendations to Engineering and Quality Control Departments for corrective action.

4. Establishes and maintains a good rapport and proper business relationship with customer plant personnel and federal and state agency personnel.

5. Contacts state and/or federal agencies to initiate corrective measures regarding quality control problems and other specifications of compliance at the request of the customer.

6. Conducts meetings with customer representatives to obtain deviations from established designs and specifications to

131

comply with federal and state regulations. Provides and interprets the above information to the Engineering Department for implementation.

7. Ensures the proper flow of required information on all programs and color changes to each operating element of the organization.

8. Maintains the current status on all approval applications with federal and state agencies as required.

Organizational Relationships

This position reports to the Director, Marketing and Sales. This position has numerous contacts with various departments from production management and quality assurance to product engineering for the explanation, interpretation, and interchange of information. Position also has numerous contacts with all customers for the above purposes.

Position Specifications

Bachelor's Degree in Mechanical Engineering or the equivalent education/work experience plus 5–7 years related work experience, including supervisory experience. Incumbent must possess a comprehensive product knowledge.

TITLE OF POSITION: **Supervisor, Customer Service**

Basic Purpose

To supervise and control the timely and accurate processing of customer releases and revisions that will contribute to production and shipments being on schedule at minimum operating and transportation cost.

Duties and Responsibilities

1. Ensures that all communications and correspondence between subordinates and customer contacts are courteous, cordial, and businesslike.

2. Plans and schedules work assignments for department personnel in accordance with priorities and objectives established by the incumbent.

3. Conducts performance evaluations of subordinate employees on a timely basis. Rewards and disciplines subordinate employees in accordance with company policies. Reviews and approves finished product shipment schedules and monitors actual shipments on a regular basis to ensure compliance with planned shipping schedules and transportation methods. Analyzes problems and recommends corrective action.

4. Evaluates and approves short- and long-range sales forecasting data prior to presentation to operating and sales management.

5. Authorizes shipment of products by premium mode of transportation in accordance with priorities and approves acceptance if premium charges are the responsibility of the company.

6. Resolves with customer contact a wide variety of problems, such as shortages or overages, shipping discrepancies, and premium transportation charges.

7. Provides and reviews shipment status reports for appropriate division personnel and analyzes and evaluates discrepancies for transmittal to Supervisor and other relevant personnel.

8. Receives cancellation information from customer and develops appropriate data regarding commitments in materials and supplies form Purchasing and Materials Departments for transmittal of cancellation claim to customer for review and payment.

9. Maintains rapport and good working relationship with appropriate customer personnel from Purchasing and Traffic Departments.

10. Visits customer facilities on an occasional basis to resolve problems associated with customer inquiries.

11. Performs other assignments that fall within the scope of this position description.

Organizational Relationships

This position reports to the Manager, Operations Services. Interacts with sales, production, accounting, data processing, and shipping personnel on a daily basis for the interchange and coordination of production and shipping information. Maintains regular communications with customers' traffic staff and represents the company when appropriate customer personnel visit the location.

Position Specifications

Bachelor's Degree in Business Administration or Transportation or the equivalent education/work experience plus 3–5 years experience in a high-volume manufacturing environment as a Customer Coordinator or Dispatcher. Must be capable of working with minimal supervision, skillful in developing solutions to day-to-day problems, and tactful in oral and written communications.

TITLE OF POSITION: **Liaison Engineer**

Basic Purpose

To provide sales and technical liaison service for the company's products for all customers, working with little or no supervision.

Duties and Responsibilities

1. Provides daily communications between appropriate division departments and customer engineering regarding the most complex design and quality control problems. Receives information from division locations concerning quality control or related problems. Uses customer drawings, material specifications, and related information to absorb problems and their ramifications fully. Contacts customer engineering personnel to explain the nature of design and quality control problems, apparent reasons as determined by division personnel, and actions to correct it. Obtains additional information from customer, summarizes, and relays to appropriate division personnel for subsequent resolution.

2. Supervises meetings between customer engineering personnel and division engineering personnel for the interchange of highly technical design and quality control information and the resolution of any subsequent problems.

3. Obtains information from customers regarding potential problem areas and contacts division personnel accordingly. Serves as liaison for subsequent resolution.

4. Meets with division tool engineering, product engineering, and quality control personnel to obtain and absorb manufacturing feasibility information of new product design by customer. Summarizes and presents this information to customer personnel, using a high degree of product knowledge.

5. Obtains cost guidance information at the request of customer engineering from division tool engineering and cost engineering. Submits reports to customer personnel accordingly.

6. Obtains prototypes and samples of company products from division locations and supplies to customer personnel as required.

7. Provides guidance to production management, quality control, and affected hourly employees for new product launch programs. This function includes explaining part usage and function, resolving deviation problems, incorporating engineering changes, and similar activities.

8. Maintains rapport and good working relationship with Customer Engineering and Purchasing Departments.

9. Assists division Cost Analysis Department in the costing of engineering changes.

10. Maintains and prepares documentation for all customer engineering changes and their effective points.

11. Coordinates and formally submits all division costing to customer for engineering changes and new product requirements.

12. Obtains and monitors customer pilot requirements for all new programs.

13. Coordinates division efforts to meet specific customer engineering requirements.

14. Provides division planning with customer requirements to assist in division marketing forecasts.

Organizational Relationships

This position reports to the Manager, Sales. Has numerous contacts with division personnel from product engineering, tool engineering, cost estimating, production management, and quality control for the explanation and interchange of information.

Incumbent will also have numerous contacts with customers' engineering and purchasing groups for above purpose.

Position Specifications

Bachelor's Degree in Mechanical Engineering or the equivalent education/work experience plus 4–6 years related work experience. Incumbent must possess a comprehensive product knowledge.

TITLE OF POSITION: **Cost Estimator**

Basic Purpose

To develop and prepare cost estimates and proposals for new company products. To evaluate and analyze engineering changes and determine appropriate cost data and related information.

Duties and Responsibilities

1. Prepares cost estimates and cost proposals for new customer products, working from drawings and related information supplied by the customer. Determines most economical manufacturing processes, methods, and sequences, required tooling, labor needs, and appropriate time values, to ensure an efficient and orderly flow of work at the plant locations.

2. Evaluates and analyzes customer and division engineering changes and determines appropriate cost data, design feasibility, and related impact, employing a comprehensive knowledge of shop methods, engineering procedures, tooling capabilities, and material applications. Communicates above information to Sales Department for subsequent evaluation.

3. Audits engineering changes that have been incorporated in the various plants and evaluates their feasibility and economic value. Makes corrective recommendations accordingly to ensure optimum efficiency, cost reduction, and productivity.

4. Conducts various studies and uses models to devise such factors as new work procedures, new equipment, new materials,

and related applications in order to evaluate the feasibility and economics of new manufacturing approaches.

5. Assists supervisor in conducting periodic audits of the division locations to determine whether proper methods, procedures, and sequences are being used in accordance with appropriate routings. Recommends corrective action to local management as necessary.

6. Ensures accuracy of cost information prior to input into computer. Audits cost master of division products and revises as necessary.

Organizational Relationships

Reports directly to the Supervisor, Cost Engineering. Has numerous contacts with division personnel from industrial engineering, purchasing, and operations for the explanation and interchange of information.

Position Specifications

Bachelor's Degree in Industrial Engineering or the equivalent in experience plus 3–5 years of practical experience in manufacturing and cost estimating. Must possess a comprehensive knowledge of design, shop methods, and engineering procedures.

VIII

Materials Management

TITLE OF POSITION: **Manager, Materials**

Basic Purpose

To plan, coordinate, manage, and control all activities related to the procurement, receipt, scheduling, storage, and inventory control movement of all direct and indirect materials, parts, and services necessary to the location in meeting its customer service commitments and other location goals.

Duties and Responsibilities

1. Develops planned materials management programs for the location requirements based on and in accordance with the automated inventory control system.

2. Plans and manages the preparation and implementation of short- and long-range inventory plans for raw materials, work in process, and finished goods to minimize material costs and meet delivery requirements of customer.

3. Oversees the preparation and implementation of short- and long-term production plans, inventory levels, and schedules that will allow the location to meet customer requirements properly while maintaining material activities at lowest possible levels.

4. Provides supervision and direction to location transportation group to ensure efficient, economic movement of transport equipment parts and materials within the plant and to ensure compliance with Department of Transportation regulations on driver records and equipment maintenance, inspection, and records.

5. Manages the purchasing activity of the location with respect to all materials, supplies, and services (direct and indirect)

and ensures that all such activities are monitored regularly for division compliance.

6. Monitors and performs periodic audits on all phases of inventory, procedures, and controls and maintains a constant awareness of status, providing for alternate plans in the event of unforeseen contingencies, including, but not limited to, work stoppages, material shortages, material rejections, new priorities, and related problems or adjustments.

7. Provides such reports as are required by the division Director, Materials and keeps division apprised of location activities as defined by procedures, policies, and parameters.

8. Analyzes and evaluates inventory and production capacities and plans in relation to current short-range and long-range commitments, and advises management as to potential delivery performance and problem areas.

9. Establishes and recommends approval of budgets for material control, production control, transportation, and purchasing sections and implements the necessary controls to keep expenditures within budget limits.

10. Ensures an effective line of communication to all local department managers and to appropriate division personnel at all times. Plans, organizes, and manages all the materials responsibility as defined by strict compliance with corporate and division policies and procedures and the scope of the location operating plan as approved.

11. Maintains a high degree of integrity and fairness in dealings and transactions with all suppliers and regularly monitors that activity to ensure its consistency.

12. Develops and maintains an effective organization through selection, training, development, compensation, and motivation of assigned personnel. Conducts merit reviews on a timely basis. Disciplines employees in accordance with division policies and procedures and local bargaining unit agreements.

13. Participates in grievance at the designated level when subordinate employees are involved. Provides background information for arbitrations as required.

14. Implements internal programs such as communications, training, work simplification, cost reduction, and other programs.

15. Prepares required reports as to progress, order status,

department budget forecasts, and miscellaneous recommendations relating to inventory and production control.

16. Manages the development of, and carrying out of, approved AAPs in the areas of EEOC compliance in accordance with the intent of Title VII of the Civil Rights Act of 1964.

17. Ensures compliance with applicable laws and regulations issued by OSHA, EPA, and other federal, state, and local regulatory agencies.

Organizational Relationships

Reports directly to the Plant Manager and functionally reports to the division Director, Materials. Has numerous contacts with manufacturing, engineering, accounting, quality control, and division sales. Reporting to this position are the supervisors of Purchasing, Inventory Control, Production Control, and Traffic.

Position Specifications

Bachelor's Degree in Business Administration or equivalent education/work experience plus 8–10 years progressive experience in materials management, including supervisory experience in purchasing, inventory control, and production control. Must display a high level of maturity and sound judgment.

TITLE OF POSITION: **Director, Purchasing**

Basic Purpose

To plan, direct, and control activities relating to the procurement of materials used in the manufacture of division products. To develop and install policies and procedures to ensure efficient operation of areas supervised consistent with corporate and division requirements.

Duties and Responsibilities

1. Directs the procurement of the division's raw materials, purchased parts, service equipment, and operating supplies at the

lowest possible price consistent with accepted standards of quality and service.

2. Develops and maintains an effective organization through selection, development, compensation, and motivation of all assigned personnel; develops managerial and other talents necessary to achieve short- and long-range objectives by effective direction, counseling, and training according to an overall manpower plan.

3. Directs subordinates in the management of their assigned responsibilities to ensure that their responsibility to meet objectives and attain satisfactory operation and performance is consistent with established policies and procedures.

4. Establishes and recommends approval of budgets for Purchasing Department. Maintains necessary controls to keep expenditures within such budgetary limitations; reviews reports from subordinates to determine expenditures as related to budgetary allowances.

5. Prepares periodic reports or other data for presentation to Vice-President, Operations indicating record of achievement on established goals, recommended improvements, personnel requirements, and other related matters.

6. Manages and maintains a balanced organization possessing flexibility, maturity, and experience in purchasing to support short- and long-range requirements effectively.

7. Directs the sale of division assets, equipment, and materials classified as obsolete or scrap under guidelines established by corporate policy and procedures.

8. Directs the development of, and carrying out of, approved AAPs in the areas of EEOC compliance in accordance with the intent of Title VII of the Civil Rights Act of 1964.

9. Negotiates major purchase agreements or arrangements considered to be of substantial value (in excess of $100,000) and/or long duration (in excess of one year) or as deemed necessary by the division President or Vice-President, Operations.

10. Establishes and monitors, through the purchasing groups, an annual cost improvement program equal to no less than a predetermined percentage of the total purchased materials per year under corporate policy and procedure.

11. Directs the supervision of the division's transportation

fleet in the movement of materials, supplies, parts assemblies, and equipment across the U.S./Canadian border in accordance with U.S. and Canadian transport regulations and in accordance with corporate transportation procedures; ensures compliance with all U.S. and Canadian customs programs.

12. Maintains various product and cost reports to identify potential areas for cost reduction efforts; performs cost studies as requested.

13. Develops and administers programs to add qualified suppliers and to encourage present suppliers to expand within guidelines of established policies.

14. Maintains contact with all markets in which the company obtains materials, and keeps the Vice-President, Operations fully advised of market status, trends, availability, and projected performance.

Organizational Relationships

This position reports to the Vice-President, Operations. Reporting to this position are two Buyers, one Secretary, and one Customs Coordinator.

Position Specifications

Bachelor's Degree in Business Administration or equivalent education/work experience plus 10–12 years experience in purchasing and materials, including experience as a Purchasing Manager, with established contacts in related markets. Must possess a high degree of maturity and integrity in conducting business affairs.

TITLE OF POSITION: **Manager, Planning and Scheduling**

Basic Purpose

To plan, schedule, and expedite production planning, scheduling, and control operations to achieve production goals and meet delivery date commitments.

143

Duties and Responsibilities

1. Participates in planning and establishing overall production objectives with consideration given to existing workload, orders, stock, parts requirements, shipping dates, and sales forecasts.

2. Organizes, formulates, and prepares master schedules to conform with delivery dates, manufacturing capacities, available manpower, and the like.

3. Expedites and coordinates detailed scheduling, machine loading, production order and routing, material requisition preparation, and the systematic release of orders to the assembly operation.

4. Maintains surveillance over orders in process to keep informed of manufacturing status and, when needed, initiates the necessary steps to maintain conformity with schedules.

5. Coordinates schedules with other departments relative to lead time required for procurement of tools and materials, subcontracting, methods and time standards development, and the like, to avoid costly delay, customer dissatisfaction, and complaints.

6. Supervises and expedites rush orders and materials that are short and revises schedules to offset delays caused by machine malfunctions, tool breakage, engineering changes, revised shipment dates, and cancellation.

7. Performs liaison with assembly, engineering, and others on matters pertaining to schedules, production, methods, materials, and designs to resolve day-to-day problems.

8. Maintains department operational procedures manual.

9. Supervises the maintenance of records and files essential to the operation.

10. Prepares required reports as to progress, order status, and department budget forecasts.

11. Coordinates the procurement of materials, components, supplies, services, and the like essential to the operation of the plant, such purchases to be of the required quality and quantity, at the most economical costs, and of timely delivery.

12. Initiates discussions with vendors concerning industry pricing trends to ensure schedules are directed to the most desirable source. Keeps division purchasing fully advised.

13. Serves as the liaison between appropriate departments of

the customers and the division regarding deviations and related quality packaging.

14. Contacts customer plants on a frequent, regular basis to establish relationships in the area of plant difficulties and related problems. Reports to affected division departments, including sales and marketing.

15. Oversees checking, packing, crating, banding, labeling, and weighing of orders for shipment.

16. Arranges for truck carriers to conform with traffic instructions and supervises the loading and bracing of products to ensure travel quality.

17. Supervises preparation of bills of lading and other forms, including shipment reports.

Organizational Relationships

This position reports to the Plant Manager. Reporting to this position are the Buyer and Expediter. Coordinates with and supports plant production, purchasing, and inventory control functions.

Position Specifications

Bachelor's Degree in Business Administration or equivalent education/work experience, plus 2–4 years experience in planning and scheduling, inventory control, internal expediting, and general supervisory work to acquire knowledge of systems, products, components, and material identities and to attain necessary proficiency.

TITLE OF POSITION: **Buyer**

Basic Purpose

To procure prototype tooling and equipment, raw materials, product purchased parts, and vendor services at the lowest possible cost consistent with accepted standards of quality and service within established time frames in the areas of new product development.

145

Duties and Responsibilities

1. Implements established policies and procedures as they relate to prototype production and raw material purchasing and recommends changes to improve performance level.

2. Prepares periodic purchase forecasts and expense budgets relative to assigned requirements.

3. Develops and administers programs to add qualified suppliers and to encourage present suppliers to expand within the guidelines of established policies.

4. Engages in detailed negotiations of pricing, delivery, service, and vendor quality as required and within limitations imposed by the purchasing procedures.

5. Reviews monthly price variances and submits recommendations on corrective action to Director, Materials.

6. Executes contractual agreements for the purchase of all tooling, materials, parts, services, and so on in new product areas, keeping the Director, Materials advised of major agreements and problem areas.

7. Maintains an energetic, complete cost reduction program on all purchasing activity and imparts this cost-saving philosophy to subordinate staff. Provides a status report on all cost savings programs, both active and proposed, and submits it monthly to the Director, Materials.

8. Maintains contact with all markets in which the company obtains materials and keeps the Director, Materials fully advised on the market status, trends, availability, and projected performance.

Organizational Relationships

This position reports to the Director, Materials. Reporting to this position is related clerical support.

Position Specifications

Bachelor's Degree in Business Administration or equivalent plus 6–8 years extensive purchasing experience in such areas as metal stamping and processing, electronics, and electronic circuitry. Must have the ability to read and understand blueprints and written detailed material specifications. Must possess a high degree of maturity and integrity in conducting business affairs.

IX

Quality Assurance

TITLE OF POSITION: **Director, Quality Assurance**

Basic Purpose

To plan, manage, and control programs and procedures to maintain an acceptable level of product quality as established by various federal, state, customer, and division requirements, including quality of purchased material, in-process material, and finished goods. To participate in the scheduling of engineering changes and production schedules as they relate to each location. To provide leadership and guidance in implementing action for quality programs and for controlling quality costs.

Duties and Responsibilities

1. Approves engineering specifications, drawings, and changes in operating manuals, and handles other approved authorizations as delegated by Vice-President, Product Assurance; ascertains that manufacturing, inspection, and test areas at all locations are working to the latest drawings.

2. Prepares periodic reports or other data for presentations to Vice-President, Product Assurance, showing record of achievement on established goals, recommended improvements, personnel requirements, and other related matters.

3. Plans and conducts periodic audits at each plant location to ensure compliance with appropriate procedures in instruction, testing, receiving, inspection, and related areas.

4. Reviews errors, spoilage, and salvage report and ensures control disposition of nonconforming material in accordance with established procedures.

5. Reviews all complaints received from customers for the purpose of determining where emphasis should be placed at

147

the plants to prevent recurrence; visits customers and suppliers periodically to confer and resolve specific quality problems.

6. Provides technical assistance to the Director, Materials in connection with the purchase of raw materials, supplies, and equipment.

7. Develops, interprets, reviews, and modifies quality plans, programs, and standards to ensure understanding and effectiveness in economic quality control of standards and quality levels.

8. Ensures compliance with applicable laws and regulations and product quality standards issued by OSHA, EPA, and other federal, state, and local regulatory agencies.

9. Maintains continuing liaison with applicable federal, state, and local agencies involved with product quality activities.

10. Obtains and evaluates technical and business data and information through membership and participation in appropriate trade and professional associations to keep superiors and other interested parties informed on current problems as they develop and pending developments that may affect the division's interests.

11. Directs the development and implementation of affirmative action programs that are in compliance with the intent of Title VII of the Civil Rights Act of 1964.

Organizational Relationships

This position reports to the Vice-President, Product Assurance. Has direct working relationship with Plant Managers and Supervisors of Quality Assurance.

Position Specifications

Bachelor's Degree or equivalent experience plus 8–10 years production or quality control experience including supervisory experience. Good overall knowledge of product quality standards, specifications, laws, and regulations established by various federal, state, and local agencies. Must have thorough knowledge of manufacturing operations, with demonstrable managerial skills in organizing, analyzing, planning, and communicating.

TITLE OF POSITION: **Manager, Quality Assurance**

Basic Purpose

To provide, implement, and administer quality assurance and control engineering functions to ensure product reliability and conformance to engineering specifications and customer/federal specifications in the most effective and economical manner possible.

Duties and Responsibilities

1. Maintains satisfaction as to quality through internal and external inspection services of raw materials, finished items purchased, and production operations and processes.

2. Conducts and/or supervises studies to determine cause, effect, and corrective measures required to remedy deviations from desirable standards of quality.

3. Confers with engineering and manufacturing personnel and in conjunction with them resolves problems of product design, specifications, materials, tooling, and production operations affecting quality.

4. Develops and maintains an effective organization through selection, training, compensation, and motivation of all assigned personnel.

5. Conducts customer and supplier visitations as required to confer on specific quality problems.

6. Reviews all customer specifications to ensure that all information is current and that all new inspection and testing are incorporated or revised.

7. Ensures establishment of and compliance with appropriate procedures in layout, testing, and other quality-assurance-related areas.

8. Provides technical assistance to division purchasing in such areas as interpretation of specifications, design concepts, and related information in connection with the purchase of raw materials, supplies, and inspection and/or test equipment.

9. Conducts periodic training sessions to keep personnel in-

formed on procedures, methods, use of equipment, and other quality assurance techniques.

10. Establishes procedures that will properly detail the inspection of component parts.

11. Reviews and evaluates all variances on component parts that do not meet prescribed tolerances and obtains deviation when required.

12. Provides technical assistance to electrical engineering section in the development of test equipment and gauges.

13. Ensures documentation and maintenance of records, drawings, and other data related to product reliability.

14. Ensures compliance with applicable laws and regulations issued by OSHA, EPA, and other federal, state, and local regulatory agencies.

15. Manages the development of, and carrying out of, approved AAPs in the areas of EEOC compliance in accordance with the intent of Title VII of the Civil Rights Act of 1964.

Organizational Relationships

This position reports directly to the Plant Manager. Coordinates activities with customers and vendors for all reliability and quality assurance standards. Provides technical assistance to manufacturing in the development of test equipment and gauges.

Position Specifications

Bachelor's Degree and/or equivalent education/work experience, including supervisory experience, plus 8–10 years experience in quality control and/or engineering. Requires comprehensive knowledge of quality control standards and procedures.

TITLE OF POSITION: **Reliability Engineer**

Basic Purpose

To carry out specialized, complex, and involved assignments of an engineering nature having to do with the development and administration of reliability procedures and techniques.

Duties and Responsibilities

1. Conducts investigative work to solve quality and/or reliability problems.

2. Conducts studies to develop inspection methods and instruments, test equipment, inspection, and sampling control procedures to ensure the control of reliability at the most economical costs.

3. Works closely with plant and division engineering, manufacturing, and inspection personnel on procedural problems involving design, methods, tooling, costs, and other areas related to the control of product quality.

4. Devises methods and designs equipment to test and evaluate both company and competitive products.

5. Assists with or personally resolves engineering problems to offset defective workmanship, material variations, or other causes of deviations from normal field performance.

6. Installs, trains personnel for, and otherwise administers new methods of inspection and new control procedures.

7. Investigates, as assigned, customers' complaints on product quality and/or reliability, and, if required, works closely with customers' representatives to resolve problems.

8. Docume ts and maintains records, drawings, and other data related to the engineering functions involved.

9. Performs failure/mode and effects analyses on each basic design of company products.

10. Does reliability program audits, math models on success diagrams, reliability allocation and prediction tests, design reviews, and test planning.

Organizational Relationships

This position reports to the Manager, Quality Assurance. Reporting to this position is one Reliability Technician. Coordinates activities with customers on all quality and reliability standards.

Position Specifications

Bachelor's Degree in Mechanical Engineering or equivalent education/work experience plus 3–5 years experience in various engineering phases, such as product and/or manufacturing engineering, quality control, and reliability engineering.

TITLE OF POSITION: **Systems Engineer**

Basic Purpose

To plan, develop, implement, and audit division reliability and quality policies that contribute to improved product reliability and minimize risk exposure through control systems, procedures, methods, and practices designed to carry out these objectives consistently, with special emphasis on the liability exposure.

Duties and Responsibilities

1. Develops, implements, and controls various reporting systems, including graphs, diagrams, and charts, concerning product controls, performance, and quality to assist top management in decision making.

2. Develops, implements, and controls systems and procedures to ensure that all disciplines that integrate product design, manufacturing, safety, and liability controls are considered. Does design reviews and maintains appropriate documentation for the various methods.

3. Develops, implements, and controls methods and procedures to monitor continuously the satisfaction of customers regarding quality and reliability.

4. Establishes and maintains a central records center for control, retention, and microfilming of quality and reliability records for all products and appropriate customer feedback.

5. Develops, implements, and controls systems to review qualification and production quality programs for the required conformance of product systems, including such information as the number of assemblies to be tested and the frequency and methods of tests.

6. Conducts supplier evaluation and capability surveys to ensure that suppliers are producing goods and services in accordance with division objectives and specifications and develops criteria and procedures for the surveys.

7. Establishes and implements revisions of procedures and

methods relating to quality assurance and reliability to ensure the use of industry's latest equipment and concepts.

8. Provides systems and procedures for tracing various aspects and histories of products, including raw materials, component parts, assemblies, location and date of manufacture, and shipment points.

9. Performs periodic audits of division operating plants and supplier facilities to ensure systems conformance, effectiveness, and accuracy and appropriate modifications of products.

10. Provides technical advice and serves as an expert witness for company's Legal Department on all litigation involving division product use and/or performance.

11. Maintains rapport and good business relationships with appropriate departments of suppliers.

12. Provides assistance to immediate superior on special assignments and programs, such as briefing plant quality control and manufacturing personnel on new programs or new test equipment and procedures and related assignments.

Organizational Relationships

Reports directly to Vice-President, Product Assurance. Provides guidance and assistance to reliability technicians at plant locations. Has numerous contacts with division personnel from quality control, manufacturing, and general management, and corporate personnel from the Legal Department to resolve reliability problems and provide litigation information. Has numerous outside contacts with customers' personnel from their Legal, Quality Control, Reliability, and Engineering Departments.

Position Specifications

Bachelor's Degree in Mechanical Engineering or the equivalent plus 6–8 years related experience. Must possess a comprehensive knowledge of company products.

TITLE OF POSITION: **Foreman, Quality Assurance**

Basic Purpose

To plan, organize, and supervise the activities of layout technicians and test and audit technicians to ensure that quality parts are released for subsequent manufacture. To analyze and evaluate variance lists to determine whether specific parts should be accepted or rejected.

Duties and Responsibilities

1. Plans and supervises the activities of the Layout and Test and Audit Departments to ensure that the dimensions of components are within tolerances prescribed by customer, government, and division specifications and standards after first piece production.

2. Analyzes and evaluates variance lists of component parts submitted by subordinates. Determines through extensive product knowledge whether minor variances would prevent the final product from being functional. Accepts or rejects the parts in accordance with the above procedure and submits reports accordingly to appropriate departments and personnel. Provides additional details to production management, tooling management, and engineering as required.

3. Reviews all reports, including inspection sheets, generated by subordinate technicians to verify proper dimensions and latest print level.

4. Schedules and organizes activities of own department in accordance with data received from production management and material control. Adjusts schedules to provide for priorities as the occasion arises. Ensures constant awareness on part of own subordinates regarding their roles in meeting these priorities.

5. Maintains a constant awareness of the status and stage of production of all jobs in own department. Provides for the reassignment of work and related necessary adjustments to meet assigned objectives when unforeseen contingencies occur,

such as machine breakdowns and other equipment failures. Coordinates these adjustments with production management, material control, and engineering.

6. Schedules vacations of subordinates so that production schedules can still be met, without interruption.

7. Reviews and signs weekly time cards.

8. Develops and maintains personnel in own department to provide an effective workforce. Rewards and disciplines employees in accordance with division policies and procedures.

9. Conducts performance reviews on a timely basis and in keeping with division guidelines. Provides training to new employees.

10. Supervises the housekeeping and proper equipment care for areas of responsibility.

11. Coordinates status of projects and related department activities with supervisory personnel of the next and/or prior shift.

12. Reviews all rejected material to ensure proper tagging and accuracy of percentage defects.

13. Documents information for special runs, including status information, completion dates, and the like.

14. Strives to reduce operating inefficiencies, absenteeism, rework time, and downtime within own sphere of responsibilities.

Organizational Relationships

Reports to the Manager, Quality Assurance. Has a wide variety of contacts with supervisory and nonsupervisory personnel from production management, material control, and engineering for the coordination of activities and resolution of problems.

Position Specifications

Position requires a high school education, plus 7–10 years of quality assurance experience. Must have comprehensive knowledge of precision tools and be able to read blueprints.

X

Research and Development

TITLE OF POSITION: **Vice-President, Research and Development**

Basic Purpose

To plan, direct, and coordinate engineering research and development functions as they relate to new products and extensive modifications or design changes in existing product lines to maintain and improve the division's marketing position, growth, and profit goals.

Duties and Responsibilities

1. Determines and plans research and development programs and objectives through joint consideration and collaboration with division management.

2. Plans, organizes, and implements programs and directives. Maintains close surveillance over procedures to effect sound application of engineering principles and adequate exploratory research to ensure an acceptable, high-quality end product.

3. Uses to the best advantage the knowledge, experience, specialties, and abilities of staff personnel and coordinates all efforts, contributions, and conclusions in scheduled sequence to obtain economic and timely results.

4. Performs liaison work with other departments, such as purchasing, manufacturing, sales, and liaison engineering, to obtain services or information pertinent to functional needs.

5. Confers with and assists staff personnel on day-to-day problems and procedures.

6. Evaluates designs, specifications, manufacturing feasibility and costs, quality and reliability test data, marketing potential, and such other facets as may be pertinent to the development of new or improved products.

7. Creates detailed engineering budgets and implements

necessary changes and adjustments caused by the marketplace and profitability requirements.

8. Establishes and maintains an effective system or project cost–performance reporting and analysis for use by Engineering, Financial, and division Managers.

9. Prepares recommendations for consideration by management as to suitability of projects; that is, which products should be researched and developed.

10. Recommends company-sponsored memberships in technical and professional societies for staff personnel.

11. Directs the development of, and carrying out of, approved AAPs in the areas of EEOC compliance in accordance with the intent of Title VII of the Civil Rights Act of 1964.

12. Develops and maintains an effective organization through the selection, development, compensation, and motivation of assigned personnel; develops managerial talents necessary to achieve short- and long-range objectives by efficient direction, counseling, and training.

13. Directs and manages a balanced organization possessing flexibility, maturity, and experience.

14. Provides technical leadership and support in all marketing efforts, including expansion of existing product applications, integration of new techniques and materials, and participation (as requested) at customer presentations to resolve current product problems.

15. Generates the most productive structure for efficient fund use within the total new budget limitation established by the profit and operational plan.

16. Provides the Research and Development Department with ready access to the latest industry information and technological data to ensure that new products represent modern materials and methods for minimum production cost.

17. Surveys manufacturing operations to implement manufacturing cost reduction programs and product improvements.

Organizational Relationships

This position reports to the President. Reporting to this position are the Managers of Product Engineering and Manufacturing Planning. Interrelates on a peer basis with the Vice-Presidents of

Operations, Product Assurance, Administration, and Business Development, and the Controller.

Position Specifications

Bachelor's Degree or equivalent experience plus 12–14 years engineering experience, including experience as a Director of Engineering. Must have a thorough knowledge of manufacturing operations in the United States, Canada, and Europe with demonstrable managerial skills in organizing, analyzing, planning, and communicating. Must have the ability to exercise good judgment in making management decisions.

TITLE OF POSITION: **Manager, Research and Development**

Basic Purpose

To plan, manage, organize, and schedule the work of design, layout, detail drafting, mode making, testing, and other related service activities associated with the development of all proposed company products.

Duties and Responsibilities

1. Confers with the Vice-President, Technical on engineering matters pertinent to the development of design drawings and specifications for new and modified products and components. Organizes, implements, and supervises project procedures, records, files, reference libraries, budget formulation, and controls. Prepares recommendations for consideration by management as to suitability of products researched and developed.

2. Assigns projects for design analysis, computer simulation, and drawing preparation and maintains close surveillance to ensure proper application of engineering principles, costs, project layout, and special part detail. Oversees the drafting of designs, layouts, and detailed part drawings and drawing changes required by engineering revisions. Oversees the reproduction, release, and distribution of prints for use in manufacturing and other division functional groups. Organizes, implements, and administers

159

the standardization of parts and the recording of specifications.

3. Performs liaison work with other departments to obtain services or information pertinent to functional needs. Collaborates with the Manager, Sales to assist in determining customers' needs and reviewing applications for special installations and adaptations.

4. Provides technical information to the Purchasing Department on matters dealing with the procurement of special materials, specifications, available sources, subcontracting, and services. Confers with and assists staff personnel on day-to-day problems and procedures. Provides engineering advice and assistance to manufacturing on production problems.

5. Evaluates designs, specifications, manufacturing feasibility and costs, quality and reliability test data, and such other technical facets as may be pertinent. Coordinates the development of sales literature, instruction books, parts lists, and similar material where technical advice and information are required.

6. Heads up various engineering projects by supervising the construction and testing of pilot models and components, competitive models, quality control checkouts, and the like at the group level.

7. Investigates prospective subcontracting sources for expediting purposes; evaluates and prepares reports as to types of machines and equipment, qualifications of workforce, and other pertinent data.

8. Assigns work to personnel engaged in the machining, fabrication, and construction of pilot models; in the mechanical and/or electrical testing of components and products; and in such metallurgical and chemical analyses as may be required.

9. Develops, supervises, and maintains own department in order to attain the required objectives. Compensates, motivates, and disciplines subordinates in accordance with division policy and procedure. Conducts merit reviews on a timely basis.

10. Carries out approved affirmative action plans in the areas of EEOC compliance in accordance with the intent of Title VII of the Civil Rights Act of 1964.

11. Ensures compliance with applicable laws and regulations issued by OSHA, EPA, and other federal, state, and local regulatory agencies.

Organizational Relationships

This position reports to the Vice-President, Research and Development. It continually interrelates with other engineering departments, quality assurance, and purchasing regarding the coordination of technical information.

Position Specifications

Bachelor's Degree in Engineering or equivalent plus 8–10 years broad engineering experience, including experience in a supervisory position.

Afterword

The concept of comparable worth will be one of the more far-reaching issues of the 1980s. Large U.S. companies are already faced with class action suits brought by women who believe that they are being discriminated against in matters of compensation through their companies' job evaluation and salary administration approaches.

Meaningful job evaluation and salary administration cannot exist, in my opinion, without a properly written job description. Job evaluation cannot exist unless some instrument is there to evaluate, nor can sound merit compensation practices be developed without directly relating the description to the performance appraisal.

Companies that will be addressing the issue of comparable worth tomorrow should develop their job descriptions today.